The Performance of Reading

CU00900763

New Directions in Aesthetics

Series editors: Dominic McIver Lopes, University of British Columbia, and Berys Gaut, University of St Andrews

Blackwell's New Directions in Aesthetics series highlights ambitious single- and multiple-author books that confront the most intriguing and pressing problems in aesthetics and the philosophy of art today. Each book is written in a way that advances understanding of the subject at hand and is accessible to upper-undergraduate and graduate students.

The Performance of Reading

An Essay in the Philosophy of Literature

PETER KIVY

Blackwell
Publishing

This paperback edition first published 2009
© 2009 Peter Kivy
Edition history: Blackwell Publishing Ltd (hardback, 2006)

Blackwell Publishing was acquired by John Wiley & Sons in February 2007. Blackwell's publishing program has been merged with Wiley's global Scientific, Technical, and Medical business to form Wiley-Blackwell.

Registered Office
John Wiley & Sons Ltd, The Atrium, Southern Gate, Chichester, West Sussex, PO19 8SQ, United Kingdom

Editorial Offices
350 Main Street, Malden, MA 02148-5020, USA
9600 Garsington Road, Oxford, OX4 2DQ, UK
The Atrium, Southern Gate, Chichester, West Sussex, PO19 8SQ, UK

For details of our global editorial offices, for customer services, and for information about how to apply for permission to reuse the copyright material in this book please see our website at www.wiley.com/wiley-blackwell.

The right of Peter Kivy to be identified as the author of this work has been asserted in accordance with the Copyright, Designs and Patents Act 1988.

All rights reserved. No part of this publication may be reproduced, stored in a retrieval system, or transmitted, in any form or by any means, electronic, mechanical, photocopying, recording or otherwise, except as permitted by the UK Copyright, Designs and Patents Act 1988, without the prior permission of the publisher.

Wiley also publishes its books in a variety of electronic formats. Some content that appears in print may not be available in electronic books.

Designations used by companies to distinguish their products are often claimed as trademarks. All brand names and product names used in this book are trade names, service marks, trademarks or registered trademarks of their respective owners. The publisher is not associated with any product or vendor mentioned in this book. This publication is designed to provide accurate and authoritative information in regard to the subject matter covered. It is sold on the understanding that the publisher is not engaged in rendering professional services. If professional advice or other expert assistance is required, the services of a competent professional should be sought.

Library of Congress Cataloging-in-Publication Data

Kivy, Peter.
The performance of reading: an essay in the philosophy of literature / Peter Kivy.
p. cm. – (New directions in aesthetics; 3)
Includes bibliographical references and index.
ISBN: 978–1–4051–4692–0 (hardback: alk. paper)
ISBN: 978-1-4051-8823-4 (papeback: alk. paper)
1. Oral interpretation. 2. Silent reading. 3. Readers' theater. I Title. II Series.
PN4145.K58 2006
808.5'5—dc22   200600179

A catalogue record for this title is available from the British Library.

Cartoon on page x by Dave Coverly. Copyright© 2005 Creators Syndicate, Inc.
By permission of Dave Coverly and Creators Syndicate, Inc.

Set in 10.5 on 12.5 pt ITC Galliard
by The Running Head Limited, Cambridge
Printed and bound in Singapore
by C.O.S. Printers Pte Ltd

01 2009

To Ed Spiegel
For Verdi, pool, and other things of almost equal importance

Contents

Are not thought and speech the same, with this exception, that what is called thought is the unuttered conversation of the soul with herself?

Plato, Sophist, trans. B. Jowett

Preface

I can't recall how the thesis of this book came to me, but I do recall when and where. I was teaching, at the time, a course in the philosophy of criticism in the arts, at my place of business, Rutgers University. The idea came to me in the midst of a class discussion, whereupon I suggested it, tentatively, to be sure, to my students. I can't recall that any of them thought it was a very good idea. And perhaps they were right. But I decided, nevertheless, to try to work the thesis out, and this is the result.

The book is, to use a somewhat old-fashioned scholarly term, a "monograph," which I take to mean a book devoted to one single subject, which it pursues in a conspicuously single-minded way. Thus, although it is, as the sub-title states, *An Essay in the Philosophy of Literature*, the reader must not expect to find treated in it the full panoply of issues the philosophy of literature comprises. I have stuck obsessively to one thing and one thing alone: the analogy that I argue for between the silent reading of literary fiction and *performance*. All else has been subjugated to that one thing. And where I have had to bring into the argument such concepts as interpretation, or the distinction between allographic and autographic arts, made famous by Nelson Goodman, I have tried to frame them in ways that will serve my own purposes, while keeping them general enough, and uncontroversial enough to be consistent with the views of a wide philosophical audience.

Of course, if the picture I attempt to draw, here, of the silent reading experience were consistent with *everyone's* beliefs about *everything* in the philosophy of literature and the philosophy of art, it would be empty: a blank canvas. If one says something that is completely uncontroversial, one says nothing at all, which is why, I suppose, the most fanatical of the Greek skeptics kept their silence.

That there are philosophical problems with my view that I have not anticipated and discussed on these pages I am certain. How could it be otherwise? But what I do not yet know about I can scarcely address here. The most I can hope for, and do hope for, is that this attempt to analogize reading with performance will open up the subject to philosophical debate. The outcome of such debate I cannot guess.

As the reader will soon see, if it has not been surmised already from the epigraph, the dominant themes of this study are provided by Plato. Much to my surprise, that arch-enemy, although admitted admirer and lover, of literary fiction has turned out to have an enormous amount to teach me about the experience of fiction-reading: indeed, *such* an enormous amount that I am tempted to call what follows a Platonic theory, even though Plato and his contemporaries experienced literary fiction very differently from the way we do in some very important respects, as we shall see. What this goes to show, which every philosopher knows already, is how immanent the philosophical past is in the philosophical present.

Work on this book, during the academic year 2004–2005, was made possible by a fellowship from the John Simon Guggenheim Memorial Foundation, and through the financial support of the Rutgers University Competitive Fellowship Leave Program. I am deeply grateful both to the Guggenheim Foundation, and to my University, for the underwriting of my project and for their confidence in my ability to complete it.

I am grateful, as well, to the people who have taken the time and trouble to read my manuscript, and to provide critical comments. Two anonymous referees for Blackwell have given me very useful suggestions. And I owe a particularly heavy debt of gratitude to Alex Neil, who has read my text with the utmost care, and provided me with perhaps the most extensive as well as the most detailed criticism that I have ever received of one of my works, prior to its publication. This book would be far poorer were it not for his unstinting labor on its behalf.

The typescript of *The Performance of Reading*, at various stages of its evolution, has been the subject of three university seminars: at the University of Wisconsin, Madison, under the direction of Noël Carroll; at the University of British Columbia, Vancouver, under the direction of Dom Lopes; and at Rutgers University, with the author presiding. I am deeply grateful to all of the participants in these seminars; and to Noël Carroll and Dom Lopes for their constructive, sympathetic criticism.

To the Rutgers graduate students, Samantha Bassler, Justin Burton, J'aimie Wells, Dennis Whitcomb, and Crystal Tychonievich, I owe a special debt of gratitude for taking time out from their incredibly busy lives to discuss my book with me. For me it was a deeply gratifying as well as intellectually fruitful experience.

I am grateful to the editor of *Philosophic Exchange*, Georges Dicker, for permission to publish material from an article in that journal, and to Dom Lopes for finding the delightful cartoon that serves as the frontispiece for my book.

Thanks are due, as well, to Eileen Power, for her always judicious and sensitive copy-editing.

Finally, I want to thank Jeff Dean, not only for his help and support, in his office as editor at Blackwell, but for his substantive philosophical comments. It is a great boon to have had an editor who is a philosopher as well. His assistance was invaluable.

As is customary, I want to take full responsibility for the mistakes I have made, while gratefully acknowledging the help of the above named.

Peter Kivy
New York City
October 2005

The Performance of Reading: An Essay in the Philosophy of Literature

1 Introduction

Common sense tells us that of the arts, some are performing arts and some are not. There are performances of musical works, but not of paintings; and there's an end on't.

Literature, in this regard, is, again according to common sense, a mixed bag. Plays are performed, novels, short stories, and narrative poems are not. And although one can read a play to oneself, or read a novel aloud as a kind of performance, even to the extent of saying the speeches as an actor would, a play is intended to be performed, a novel or short story or narrative poem to be silently read, full stop (as the English say).

Common sense is right, of course, to the extent that it remains at a suitable viewing distance, and remains suitably coarse-grained. Someone who sold tickets to a performance of *Hamlet* or Beethoven's Ninth Symphony would be considered by common sense, quite correctly, to be acting in a wholly rational, intelligible way. Whereas if someone were to attempt a sale of tickets to his *silent* reading of *Pride and Prejudice*, he would be considered by common sense to be either mad, or some kind of conceptual artist "making a point." And common sense would be right.

But common sense does not necessarily have the last word over philosophy in this regard if we focus down, and hone our conceptual apparatus. To that end, I intend to pursue analogies between reading and performance: in particular, between reading to oneself novels and stories, and performing or experiencing performances of musical works. In doing so I hope to discover some things about our appreciation of silently read literary works, and, in the end, to show that reading and performance have more in common than common sense suspects. This is not, I should add, a *normative* claim, about how we *should* read fictional works, but a *descriptive* claim about how we, at least some of us, *do* read them. It is an exercise in analysis, not legislation.

2 A Little Ontology

Perhaps a good starting point might be the ontology of art works. In *Languages of Art*, the late Nelson Goodman made a distinction between what he called "allographic" and "autographic" arts, which is now in standard use among analytic philosophers of art.[1] The paradigm instance of autographic art is the art of painting. When a painter produces his kind of art work, it is a solitary, easily identifiable physical object, located in both spatial and temporal dimensions. There may be fake *Mona Lisas*, but there is only one, *echt Mona Lisa*.

By contrast, music, at least in the West and in the modern era, is an allographic art. The musical work, Beethoven's Fifth Symphony, unlike the *Mona Lisa*, does not seem to be a solitary, easily identifiable physical object located in both spatial and temporal dimensions. Beethoven's Fifth Symphony cannot be picked up, carried away, or, in any obvious way destroyed, the way the *Mona Lisa* clearly *can* be. Furthermore, unlike the *Mona Lisa*, Beethoven's Fifth Symphony can seemingly defy the ontological interdict against being in two difference places at the same time since, clearly, it can be performed in New York City by the New York Philharmonic Orchestra at the very same time it is being performed in Boston by the Boston Symphony Orchestra.

Goodman himself thought that a musical work like Beethoven's Fifth Symphony is what he called a class of compliants with the score.[2] Every performance of a musical work is a score compliant – that is to say, fulfills the conditions the score lays down for being a performance of *that* work – and the musical work simply *is* the sum total of all its performances, past, present, and to come. Thus, put succinctly, every musical work is a compliance class.

Goodman's analysis of the musical work has problems very familiar to philosophers of art; and it would be beside the point to canvass them here. Without, therefore, arguing the matter, I am going to adopt, for the present discussion, a Platonic analysis of the musical work, and the work/performance relation. Platonism, of course, has its own repository of problems. But they too are, for present purposes, beside the point.

On the Platonic analysis of musical works like Beethoven's Fifth Symphony, they are universals or types, of which their performances are instances or tokens. According to "extreme Platonism," musical works are "discovered" types, as would be the case with the usual Platonist account of mathematical objects.[3] According to "qualified Platonism," works are "created" types.[4] But on both views the relationship between work and performance is much the same. And that is all that matters here.

Turning now to literature, it would appear that drama is among the allographic arts, and that its analysis, along Platonic lines, closely parallels that of music. The written text of the play is the "score" of the work; a performance of the play is a "score compliant," and token of the type.

Now as a matter of fact things are not that simple. For something stands between a particular performance, say, of *Hamlet*, and Shakespeare's work: it is, for example, John Gielgud's production. The production, cum direction, scenery, the entire *mise-en-scène*, is itself a version of the work, a token of the type; and the performance on a particular Saturday matinee is a token of the type "John Gielgud's production of Shakespeare's *Hamlet*," the Saturday evening performance another token of that type. And, of course, Laurence Olivier's production of *Hamlet* is *another* version of Shakespeare's play, another token of that type; but, as well, a type in its own right, of which the various individual performances are tokens.

But, actually, the very same complication exists in the musical work/performance relation, although not so obviously, even if there is only one performer involved. Thus, Vladimir Horowitz's performance, on some particular Saturday afternoon, of Chopin's *Revolutionary Etude*, is a token of the type which is Chopin's work. However, Horowitz, in a given year, performed the *Revolutionary Etude* numerous times. And each of these performances was quite recognizable to expert ears as a token of the type "Horowitz's version of the *Revolutionary Etude*" (at least until such time as he might have seen fit to change his interpretation of the work radically enough to constitute a different Horowitz version of it). Thus, the type "Horowitz's version of the *Revolutionary Etude*" stands between the type, *Revolutionary Etude*, and the token, Horowitz's performance of the *Revolutionary Etude* on a given Saturday afternoon in 1950, as the type "Gielgud's production of *Hamlet*" stands between Shakespeare's *Hamlet* and a performance of Gielgud's production of *Hamlet* on a given Saturday afternoon in 1950.

Nevertheless, given this complication, it is still true to say that Horowitz's performance of the *Revolutionary Etude* on a given Saturday afternoon in 1950 is a token of the type Chopin's *Revolutionary Etude*, as a performance of Gielgud's production of *Hamlet* is a token of the type Shakespeare's *Hamlet*. And I will continue to talk that way in what follows.

3 A Little More Ontology

Turning now to read literature, which is my major topic, I will talk for a while of Jane Austen's *Pride and Prejudice*, merely by way of example.

Now, clearly, novels and short stories are examples of allographic art. What kind of examples they are is not so obvious.

What *is* obvious is that *Pride and Prejudice*, like Beethoven's Fifth Symphony, is not a physical object, located in spatial and temporal dimensions, at least for the extreme *or* the moderate Platonist. You can no more pick up, carry away, or destroy the novel than you can the symphony. It would appear that the novel is a type. But what are its tokens?

You have your copy of *Pride and Prejudice*, I have mine. But, I would urge, our copies of the novel are not tokens of the type *Pride and Prejudice*, any more than our scores of Beethoven's Fifth Symphony are tokens of the type Beethoven's Fifth Symphony. All of the many copies of *Pride and Prejudice* are tokens of a type, but that type is not the work: it is the notation of the work. Likewise with all of the many copies of the Fifth Symphony.

Furthermore, *Pride and Prejudice* does not *seem*, anyway, to have the same ontology as such other literary works as *Hamlet* or *Ghosts*, because, as I said at the outset, common sense has it that drama is a performing art and the novel is not. Of course, there may be copies of *Hamlet* and *Ghosts*, but these are no more tokens of the types, *Hamlet* and *Ghosts*, than the copies of the score are tokens of the type Beethoven's Fifth Symphony, or the copies of *Pride and Prejudice* tokens of the type *Pride and Prejudice*. The tokens of the types *Hamlet* and *Ghosts* are their performances (as qualified above) as are the tokens of the type Beethoven's Fifth Symphony. But the novel is not, by hypothesis, a performing art. So whatever *its* ontology, it does not seem that it can be the work-type/performance-token ontology. So where do we go from here?

Well I think it pretty obvious that the answer is going to be: the novel is a reading art, and so it trivially follows that the tokens of the type *Pride and Prejudice* are its readings: your reading is one, my reading is another; and if I read it twice those are two tokens of the type. Needless to say, I do not think this answer is obvious in the sense of needing no further argument for its establishment. Indeed, the entire monograph to follow is its argument. But perhaps it is more correct to say that it is the most obvious *candidate*, and this has not gone unnoticed, as we shall see, although no previous writer, so far as I am aware, has ever given this candidate a run for the money. That is what I intend to do.

"Reading," of course, has a double meaning in these contexts, and it is of vital importance to what follows that we get this straight. There is the sense of "reading," which I was assuming in the last paragraph, where what is being referred to is the specific event of, say, my first reading of *Pride and Prejudice*. This event took a certain specifiable amount of time. And, as most people, myself included, do not read novels at one sitting, I shall assume that the reading of a novel is not one uninterrupted event, but the sum total of a number of reading events, separated by various, sometimes protracted periods. Indeed, I would go so far as to say that reading a novel at one go is not only unusual, and in some cases impossible, but contrary to authorial intention, and, consequently, not the most artistically correct way of experiencing such works. I will argue this point at length later on, and will only remind the reader at this point that many of the novels of Dickens and other great novelists of the nineteenth century appeared serially in literary periodicals, and hence *could not* be read at one go, unless you waited for all the installments to be published, nor, arguably, were they intended to be.

This sense of reading, that I am now discussing, is, as I have said, an event taking up a certain non-continuous period of time. It is the kind of event we would describe as an act or an activity: it is an action performed by a reader. And the most important aspect of this act is that it is, or results in an "experience." The point of an act of reading *Pride and Prejudice* is to have an experience of it for the usual reasons people have for experiencing works of art of that kind. Some people might say that such a reading act has as its purpose the experiencing of the work "aesthetically." But I will not say that. I will say rather that its purpose (usually) is the experiencing of it *qua* art work of that kind: all the art-relevant ways of experiencing it, of which the aesthetic way is one.

The second sense of "reading" I have in mind is the sense in which a "reading" of a novel is synonymous with an "interpretation" of it. Thus two literary critics might have, as we would say, two different "readings" of *Pride and Prejudice*, meaning that they interpret it in different ways. There is, to be sure, an intimate relation between the two senses; and I will be discussing interpretation later on. At this point it seems advisable simply to stipulate that I shall mean by a "reading" things like my first reading of *Pride and Prejudice*, or your re-reading of it, and use "interpretation" for the other sense of "reading." In the rare case in which I depart from this usage it will be altogether obvious.

What I am suggesting, then, to bring out the major thesis of this section, is that the ontology of read literary works is the type/token ontology of musical and dramatic works. But whereas the tokens of music, drama, and the other performing arts are performances, the tokens of read literary works are readings. I now want to go on to elaborate further on this thesis.

4 Early Experiences of Literature

The type/token ontology works for the novel, as well as for drama and music. Furthermore, the best candidates for a novel's tokens appear to be its readings, whereas the *obvious* candidates for the tokens of plays and musical works are their performances. This *suggests*, at least, that it might be philosophically illuminating to pursue an analogy between readings and performances.

But which way should the analogy go? Should we try to illuminate the nature of readings by showing in what ways they are analogous to performances (besides the obvious way of their both being tokens of work-types) or should we try to illuminate the nature of performances by showing in what ways they are analogous to readings? I might just arbitrarily decide to try one rather than the other to see what results I get. However, there is a more rational way of making the decision. *Read* literature is a comparatively late development in the history of the Western literary arts. It, I shall argue, "comes out of" performed literature; and I think it is a reliable precept that we can frequently learn about a thing or a practice by learning about its origins and history. I am well aware of the danger, in this regard, of committing the genetic fallacy of inferring that something must have certain properties or a certain character merely because its historical predecessors and sources had those properties or that character. I shall try very hard not to commit the genetic fallacy. Certainly I am not saying that readings are performances, just because I *am* saying that read literature had its historical origins in performed literature. Anyone who draws an analogy between two things, as I am doing, obviously is acknowledging that they are not the same thing: one cannot analogize something with itself; or, in other words, analogy presupposes non-identity.

Another danger of my procedure, besides that of falling into the genetic fallacy, is committing the fallacy, if that is the right name for it, of doing "armchair history." I am not a literary historian, a cultural historian, or any other kind of historian. That being the case, any historical statements I make are at best highly suspect, and should be treated as such. Nevertheless, I shall try very hard to make historical claims only of the most obvious and (I hope) uncontroversial kind. And all I can do to guard against historical error is to keep my fingers crossed (and maybe you might do the same with yours). But let me just add, for those who are strongly suspicious of *a priori* history (and rightly so) that even if most of my historical speculations are mistaken, the general thesis of this book will not be invalidated on that account alone. It will simply have to rest on a less weighty evidential base.

Let's start at the beginning. The oldest texts in the Western literary canon that are more or less widely read are the Homeric epics.[5] We read them in our easy chairs, in modern, paperback translations, but we hardly need reminding that that is not how they were experienced in their own time, or in classical Greek culture. They were both part of an oral tradition, and were, I like to think, recited (or sung?) around the campfire while the jug was being passed. However that may be, what we do know is that they weren't read but "performed." And since, presumably, there were no written texts, the work/performance, type/token ontology, if it applies at all, applies more loosely than in regard, say, to the nineteenth-century novel. The poems must have been in a continual state of flux, contributed to by many hands, so it would be hard to separate performance from work (although empirical research on living "storytellers" reveals that a very long narrative can be repeated over and over again with remarkable accuracy and little change, in the complete absence of a written text).

Where my real interest in the Homeric epics begins, and where they begin to have real significance for my argument is when, between approximately 750 and 700 BC the Greek texts, more or less as we know them, were written down and divided into the familiar 24 "books" of the *Iliad* and *Odyssey*.

Once we have written texts we of course have the type/token ontology in place. However, philosophers know, from Plato's dialogues, the *Ion* and *Republic*, that the tokens were not readings but "performances." The Homeric epics, and other Greek poetry that we naturally now experience as read texts, were apparently experienced in Plato's Greece as recited or sung. Poetry for the Greeks, it would seem, was a performance art even when it was not, as it was in the case of the tragedies and comedies, a staged performance, and even when, as in the case of the *Iliad* and *Odyssey*, there was an established, authoritative text.

What kind of performances were these? We know from Book III of the *Republic* that the recitations of Homer and the others were, to say the least, very "lively." Plato's descriptions may be more than somewhat hyperbolic, since his intent was to ridicule these performances so as to cast them in a bad light, both morally and epistemically. But if his account is to be at all credited, they must have involved quite a display of virtuosity, however misplaced Plato may have thought this virtuosity was.

Plato's idea of what the "model" performer of poetry should be is of one whose "style will be both imitative and narrative; but there will be very little of the former, and a great deal of the latter."[6] What Plato means here is that there is, in Homer, for example, both straight narration and quotational "speeches." The performer, then, in his singing or reciting of Homer plays two parts, as it were. He plays the part of the fictional or authorial narrator (and more of that later on) and he plays the parts of the characters whose speeches are quoted in the narrative. And because Plato thought playing the parts of characters, if they are wicked or unvirtuous ones, is bad for the performer, as is any other form of "imitation," he advised performers to, as much as possible, steer clear of enacting the dramatis personae and stick to straight narration. For "a just and good man in the course of narration comes on some saying or action of another good man – I should imagine that he will like to personate him . . . .. But when he comes to a character which is unworthy of him he will not make a study of that . . . ."[7]

The sort of performer that Plato deplores, and, I suspect, was the more commonly met with

> will narrate anything; and the worse he is the more unscrupulous he will be; nothing will be beneath him: moreover he will be ready to imitate anything, not as a joke, but in right good earnest, and before a large audience. As I was just now saying, he will attempt to represent the roll of thunder, the noise of wind and hail, or the creaking of wheels and pulleys, and the various sounds of flutes, pipes, trumpets, and all sorts of instruments: also he will bark like a dog, bleat like a sheep, and crow like a cock; his entire art will consist in imitation of voice and gesture and there will be very little narration.[8]

I am far from knowing just how accurately Plato has represented the performers of the Homeric epics in his day. Be that as it may, whether you experienced it sung or recited by Plato's puritanical practitioner, or by the one who is "ready to imitate anything," it is clear that you were experiencing one of the performing arts, just as surely as if you were attending a tragedy by Sophocles, even if, in the poetry recitation, one man performed all of the parts.

But there is another aspect of the poetry performance that comes out in the *Ion*, which will seem to the modern reader perhaps even more odd than a reciter of Homer who imitates "the creaking of wheels and pulleys" and will "bleat like a sheep." Ion, after whom the little dialogue is named, pursues the profession of "rhapsode." He sings the poetry of Homer, to the accompaniment, it would seem, of a lyre. (Socrates specifically refers to Ion's skill on this instrument.) He narrates the story and speaks the speeches, though whether he also creaks and bleats is not mentioned.

What is very interesting about Ion, and is in fact the main topic of the dialogue, is that he is a *specialist*. The *only* poet he performs well is Homer. That is not in itself odd, I suppose, to us, for we are quite happy with the notion that an actor be a pre-eminent Shakespearean, but not as good as someone else at Eugene O'Neill or Arthur Miller.

What *is* odd is that what Ion is good at, as well, in regard to Homer, is speaking *about* Homer, and that speaking about Homer *may be part of his performance* (although, as we shall see, this is not by any means a certainty).

Socrates tells us that "no man can be a rhapsode who does not understand the meaning of the poet. For the rhapsode ought to interpret the mind of the poet to his hearers, but how can he interpret him unless he knows what he means?"[9] There is nothing odd-sounding here, because we would all agree, I am sure, that you can't make a good performance of a poet unless you understand what the poet is talking about. (Whether you can make a performance *at all*, even a bad one, is, of course, another question.) And when Socrates says that the rhapsode's job is to "interpret the mind of the poet to his hearers," we understand him to mean that the rhapsode or actor interprets the mind of the poet to his hearers *through* his performance of the narration and speeches.

But that, apparently, is not what Socrates means. For Ion responds to Socrates' comment: "Very true, Socrates; interpretation has certainly been the most laborious part of my art; and I believe myself able to speak about Homer better than any man . . .."[10] And Socrates responds to Ion in kind, later on referring to Ion's Homeric "gift" as "The gift you have of speaking excellently about Homer . . .."[11] So it appears that what Socrates means when he says that "the rhapsode ought to interpret the mind of the poet to his hearers" is that he ought to "speak about Homer" to his hearers, and that indeed is what Ion has taken him to mean all along.

That I think is what has to seem odd to the modern reader. For if I am understanding Plato correctly on this point in the *Ion*, then the Greek rhapsode in his performance of the Homeric epics not only recited or sung the narration, and the characters' speeches, perhaps impersonating the dramatis personae with gesture and voice; he also, *in his performance*, made interpretive remarks about the meanings of the poems he was performing. It is as if between a performance of the first and second acts of *Hamlet*, one of the actors should step forward onto the apron and give a discourse on the reason for Hamlet's delayed revenge, and the possibility of an Oedipal relationship between Hamlet and Gertrude; and if the actor did that, surely his discourse would not be part of the performance but an interruption of it. However, when Ion performed the *Iliad* and *Odyssey*, apparently, part of his performance consisted in *telling*, not showing his audience what it was that Homer was trying to convey; what Homer really meant. In other words, Ion *performed* what we would think of as literary criticism.

When I first read the *Ion*, and each time I have reread it in the past, I have found this "critical" aspect of the rhapsode's performance not only exceedingly odd, but almost incomprehensible. What is this all about? What sort of experience would it be, of a story-telling, interlarded with remarks like, "Now here I think Homer is trying to convey to us the moral price one must pay for the act of vengeance," and others of that kind? Or is that really what Plato is telling us was going on? Wouldn't one find such critical interpolations a disturbing and unwelcome interruption of the narrative flow? What kind of literary institution are we encountering here? The whole thing sounds incredible, given our understanding both of the performing and of the reading arts.

Well, I think I am now beginning to find what the Greek rhapsodes seem to have been doing in this regard to be far more comprehensible than I once thought it. Indeed, not only do I now find it comprehensible in its ancient context, I am beginning to believe that it still survives in the modern reading experience, albeit in an appropriately modified form. And I am not speaking here about the modern literary critic, although that personage does play a role. I am talking about something far different. And what that is is another promissory note I am taking out, to be paid in full later on. Before that there are other points to consider.

5 Reading to Yourself

I have been arguing, in the previous section, that a reading of the *Ion* and Book III of the *Republic* reveals that for the Greeks of Plato's time, and, I think we have a right to assume, for an extended period of time thereafter, non-dramatic fiction, or at any rate, what *we* regard as non-dramatic fiction, of which the Homeric epics are the prime exemplars, was experienced as a performance art. To this the skeptic might reply that the evidence advanced hardly warrants such a sweeping conclusion. After all, *we* have public poetry readings. That doesn't mean we don't, more often than not, experience poetry by reading it to ourselves. As a matter of fact, private reading is our usual way.

But two additional considerations will, I think, bolster the more sweeping conclusion of the previous section, that non-dramatic fiction, which is to say, fictional poetry, was indeed, largely, a performing art for the ancient Greeks. Before I get to that, however, a word is necessary about my use of the terms "fiction" and "fictional" in this context. Obviously the Greek epics and tragedies are fiction *to us*. For large numbers of Greeks, perhaps, they may have been taken for historical narrative and theological truth. Myth for us, history for them. Nevertheless, I shall, even when I am talking about the ancient Greek experience of these literary works, not our experience of them, continue to use the terms "fiction" and "fictional." For nothing I say will turn on the question. Whatever the ancient Greeks may have thought about the historical and theological reality of these stories, they surely experienced them as narratives; and what I have to say about the reading experience, at least for now, is neutral with regard to historical or theological truth and falsity, or the *intention* to write poetic-ally true rather than poetically fictional stories.

Furthermore, I should add that the concept of fiction must be kept sep-arate from the concept of truth, in the following respect: that something is "fiction" in the sense of "literary fiction" does not imply falsehood. Someone can, of course, make up a story – that is what fiction amounts to – but have it end up (accidentally) true, which is why, of course, works of fiction begin with the official disclaimer to the effect that "this is a work of fiction and any similarity of its characters to persons living or dead is purely coincidental." Thus, even though, in ordinary language, one is prone to say, "that is pure fiction, there is not a particle of truth in it," when it comes to the *literary* sense of "fiction," truth is not the determin-ing ground.

So, to get back to the main point, why should we think that the ancient Greeks didn't, like us, generally experience poetic fiction as a read experi-ence, even though, again like us, they also went to poetry recitations by such performers as Ion the rhapsode? The answer is twofold.

To begin with, it is pretty well known that until the invention of the printing press, and, indeed, even until well after that, the owning of books could not have been widespread, nor, of course, at least in medieval Europe, was literacy. How many ancient Greeks owned books? And how many books might a single person own?

Socrates tells us in the *Phaedo* that when he heard about Anaxagoras' doctrine of the world's being directed by "mind," he immediately acquired all of that philosopher's "books," so that he could read about the doctrine at first hand. And I am sure that Socrates, Plato, Aristotle, and their well-born friends owned and read books. But my conjecture is that the availa-bility of books could not have been great, and the ownership of them not widespread. In which case, and, again, this is sheer conjecture, most Athe-nians experienced the poetic fiction of Homer and the rest in the only way readily accessible to them: the public performances of the "professional" rhapsodes. And if this is not true of Socrates, Plato, Aristotle, and their circle, it was true of the citizenry at large.

As well, it must be observed that reading to yourself, "silent reading," is a rather late development in the history of literacy. When Socrates read the works of Anaxagoras to himself, he read them *aloud* to himself. And this is no mere conjecture, for Socrates himself tells us in the *Phaedo* that he first discovered the books of Anaxagoras when he "*heard* [not saw] someone reading, as he said, from a book of Anaxagoras . . .."[12]

As far as I know, the first mention of silent reading is in Saint Augustine's *Confessions*, in a passage celebrated for just that reason. So when Aristotle says in the *Poetics*, where he is comparing tragic drama with epic poetry, that tragedy can have its full effect, its "vividness in reading as well as in performance,"[13] he should not be taken to mean reading the way we envision it. When Aristotle read the Greek tragedies, he read them audibly, not "in his head." (The library at Alexandria must have been a pretty noisy place.)

Well, what of it? Simply this: that even in the, I think, less common experience of fictional poetry, where the Greek citizen might read "to himself," rather than attend a rhapsode's performance, he was attending a performance nonetheless – *his own performance.*

A pretty minimal performance, you might say, hardly worthy of the name. But I do not think it can be dismissed so lightly.

Do you ever read aloud to yourself? I do, when I want to try out a passage I have just written, for smoothness and continuity, or when I want to hear how a passage of poetry sounds. And when I do read a passage aloud, I tend, quite naturally, even without trying, to read it "with expression," as if for an audience. Indeed, what requires trying, what requires effort is to read *without* expression. I trust this is the same with everyone.

But if this is true of you and me, in a silent reading culture, even when reading aloud quite mundane, scholarly prose, how much more so must it have been in a culture where silent reading was virtually unknown, and what was being read was Homer and Hesiod. Now I am not suggesting for a moment that an educated Athenian, when he read the *Iliad* aloud to himself, imitated the creaking of pulleys and the bleating of sheep, and declaimed the speeches in the manner of John Barrymore. I do suggest that he did not read in a monotone, like a court recorder. I suggest that he could not have avoided, nor would he have wanted to avoid, an expressive reading in which what we would hear, and what he would hear, and what he heard, was, if you like, a minimal performance, but a real performance for all of that.

In trying to imagine to myself what kind of thing I am talking about here I think the most helpful analogy is to, for example, an amateur pianist, playing to herself, for her own pleasure, say, a Beethoven sonata. Part of her pleasure derives from her activity of playing, to be sure; but another part of course is in the *hearing* of what she is playing. The pianist is hearing a performance of the Beethoven sonata put on by herself. Likewise, I suggest, for the Greek reading Homer to himself aloud.

Thus, given how few people would have had access to books in the ancient world, few people could have experienced fictional literature in any way but as a performance. This was the normal way to experience it. And perhaps it might have been as rare for someone to experience Homer by reading the text to himself as it is now for someone to experience Beethoven by playing it to herself or reading the score. (More, much more about score-reading later on.)

Furthermore, even if you were one of the few "intellectuals"(?) or "aristocrats"(?) who did possess written texts and did read Homer and Hesiod to yourself, it would not be the way Brahms read the score of *Don Giovanni* to himself but the way he played a Beethoven sonata to himself. You would have read it out loud to yourself, "with expression," I think, and would have been the sole audience to it, but audience nevertheless, to your own performance.

The notion of performing to oneself may perhaps raise some skeptical eyebrows, as the notion of duties to oneself has done in moral theory. Is there something "odd," even amounting to a "category mistake," in suggesting that someone can perform a piano sonata to herself, or recite a poem aloud to herself as a performance?

In this regard it would be well to turn to Gilbert Ryle, the philosopher who put the concept of the "category mistake" on the philosophical map, and who had some relevant skeptical remarks to make on the reflexive phrase, "to oneself." He wrote, in one of his last essays, "Thought and Soliloquy":

> We look through his caravan window and see the circus clown or the conjuror going through his capers or his prestidigitations in solitude. I suppose we *might*, though I doubt if we really would say that he is clowning or conjuring to himself, but can he literally be amusing or mystifying himself in the way in which he will be amusing or mystifying the children this evening? . . . Here there can be no doubt. They are not trying to amuse or mystify an audience, however small. They are, in privacy or by themselves, going through the moves of their tricks, because they are either trying to think up new tricks, or rehearsing their tricks, or both together, in order to be able and ready to amuse or mystify the children when they perform these very same operations this evening.[14]

The argument, on first reflection, seems to be persuasive. But we must beware of being steamrolled. There is nothing here to suggest that "performing to himself" has any of the paradoxical flavor of "amusing or mystifying himself . . .."

Ryle has placed heavy emphasis on the fact that the clown and conjuror are "rehearsing" their acts. But because that is their *overall* purpose, it does not follow that they are not also *performing* to themselves. If I say that someone is unscrewing a nut and you reply that, no, he is changing a tire, the silliness of your response would be pretty obvious. The act of unscrewing the nut is obviously part of a larger act of changing the tire. So the question is not, in the present instance, What is the clown doing, performing to himself or rehearsing his act?, any more than it is a question whether the tire-changer is unscrewing a nut or changing a tire. They both are doing both. The real question is whether it is absurd, even a category mistake, to say that in rehearsing his act, the clown is performing to himself. What I would like to urge is that, indeed, it would be absurd to say that he is *not* performing to himself.

When you rehearse, you of course must evaluate what you are doing, so that you can correct what is wrong, preserve what is right. You *must* be your own audience. That is what you do when you rehearse your soliloquy or your sonata in private. Nor is there anything in the least paradoxical in saying that the actor or the pianist was pleased or displeased by his recital or playing. Furthermore, there is nothing paradoxical in describing what the actor and the pianist are doing as performing, nothing paradoxical in describing each his own audience. In rehearsing, performance (to oneself) is to rehearsal what nut-unscrewing is to tire-changing.

But what of Ryle's claim that it is absurd to describe the clown as amusing himself or the conjuror as mystifying himself? Well that really is something of a red herring for us. It may well be some kind of category mistake to talk of mystifying oneself; there is, at least, something problematic about such talk. It seems as if we have here a close relative of lying to oneself or deceiving oneself; and there are, as is well known, conceptual problems surrounding both. There is no need, however, for us to open that can of worms. Suffice it to say that there very well may be some things that you can't do to yourself. Ryle adduces various examples: "But I cannot literally fence with myself, resuscitate myself, outlive myself, or insult, compliment or trick myself."[15] And so on.

All well and good. *But* there are lots of things you *can* do to or for yourself, and performing is one of them. I think we *would* say that the clown and the conjuror are performing to themselves; and if that implies the clown is clowning to himself, and the conjuror conjuring to himself, then Ryle is mistaken in doubting that we would say that they were doing those things, although we might very well stop at saying the clown is amusing himself and the conjuror mystifying himself. (As for the former, however, it might be remembered that the joke-teller frequently laughs at his own jokes.) Of course, in performing to yourself there are many things you *can't* do, among them those things that you can't do to or for yourself. Perhaps mystifying and surprising yourself are among them. That is all the same to us. What we need, merely, is the conclusion that one way you can experience and enjoy a poem is to recite it, which is to say, perform it to yourself, one way you can experience and enjoy a piano sonata is to play it, which is to say perform it, to yourself. And nothing Ryle says about clowns and conjurors seems in any way to cast doubt on that conclusion.

From these considerations I want to conclude that in the ancient world, the experience of fictional literature, even of the non-dramatic kind, would have been the experience of a performing art, whether you were part of an audience, listening to the rhapsode perform, or whether you were reading to yourself (in which case listening to yourself perform). And with this conclusion now established, I want to push my "conjectural history" of the experience of literary fiction forward to the question of when this experience took on its modern form of "curling up with a good book" and *reading*, not performing, *to yourself.*

6 Not Moving Your Lips

It seems a pretty safe bet that literacy, if anything, decreased in the Middle Ages, and that for most people, if fictional literature was experienced at all, it was experienced in song and recitation.

Was *Canterbury Tales* experienced, generally, as recited or read? By this time silent reading may have been firmly in place. But who knows how extensive it really was? Its first recorded mention, as I have said, is in the *Confessions* of Saint Augustine (written between 397 and 398 AD), where, in the crucial passage which tells of his conversion, Augustine writes: "I had put down the book containing Paul's Epistles. I seized it and opened it, *and in silence* I read the first passage on which my eyes fell."[16] That Augustine took pains to mention that he read the passage "in silence" of course strongly suggests that silent reading was then a very uncommon practice. In any event, it seems certain that we are here not yet in a "silent reading culture," if that implies widespread literacy and the proliferation of books.

For those who first come to know that in the ancient world everyone who read read *aloud*, as I did not too very long ago, it seems almost incomprehensible as well as incredible. But the fact is that at that time there were but two ways for you to "read" a text: hear someone else read it to you, or hear yourself reading it aloud to yourself. Reading *silently* to yourself was simply unknown. Not only *wasn't* it done; it *couldn't* be done in the circumstances then obtaining.

Nor are we talking here merely about the experience of poetry and drama, as I was doing above, but about *all* texts whatever, from philosophy and cosmology to personal letters and official documents. It is, for example, perfectly clear that Plato's dialogues, as well as Aristotle's works, were meant for "performance." As Gilbert Ryle puts the point: "Dialogues are exoteric since they are recited to the general public. Lectures are not exoteric since they are delivered to students in the school."[17] But the bottom line is that *neither* was written for the single lone reader.

That notwithstanding, there would seem to be no reason to infer that because Plato wrote his dialogues for oral, dramatic presentation, they were not also perused in private by solitary readers, as are plays today; nor, furthermore, would there seem to be any reason to infer that they were not sometimes read silently when read in private, as we read today.

Well, there is no reason to believe that folks in the ancient world did not read texts alone to themselves, in private, although the scarcity of manuscripts strongly indicates that this was the unusual rather than the usual way of doing things. But there is a *conclusive* reason, apart from the statements of such authors as Plato and Augustine, quoted above, for believing that *all* reading, private no less than public, was reading aloud. Ancient texts were written in what is known to linguists and paleographers as *scriptura continua*, which is to say, uninterrupted writing. What this means is that in ancient writing *there was no separation between words*. And because there was no separation between words, it was, quite literally, impossible for the ancient reader to read silently with comprehension, even if he had wanted to do so. As Paul Saenger puts the point in his remarkable book, *Space Between Words: The Origins of Silent Reading*: "In these circumstances, the ancient reader in his initial preparation or *praelectio* of a text normally had to read orally, aloud or in a muffled voice, because overt physical pronunciation aided the reader to retain phonemes of ambiguous meaning . . ... The aural retention of inherently ambiguous fragments often was essential until a full sentence was decoded."[18]

This, then, was how Plato and Aristotle, and those before them, read in the ancient Mediterranean world. Theirs was an oral and aural culture when it came to comprehension – the reading – of texts, whether poetry or prose, fictional or factual. All reading then was, in this sense, performance or the audition of performance.

Nor did this aspect of reading culture in the West change in an appreciable way until the late Middle Ages. And it *did* change only with the development of the modern text: in particular, the custom of putting spaces between words. "The importance of word separation by space is unquestionable, for it freed the intellectual faculties of the reader, permitting all texts to be read silently, that is, with eyes only."[19]

Apparently the first to space words in their manuscripts, in the middle ages, were the Insular scribes of the seventh century. "The origins of rapid, silent reading lie in the scribal techniques and grammatical teachings that developed in Ireland and England in the seventh and eighth centuries. The first separated Latin manuscript books in western Europe were Irish . . .."[20] But the Continent was far later in adopting spaces between words. And it was not, according to Saenger, until the thirteenth century that, throughout the West, "the silent reading of word-separated texts was a normal practice of literate society";[21] and other scholars put it later than that. Indeed, according to one, "It was only towards the close of the 19th century that it became a common practice in Europe to read silently."[22]

Furthermore, it should be borne in mind that even when, as Saenger puts it, silent reading was a *normal* practice of literate society, that does not mean it was necessarily the *usual* practice. Indeed, the orality of poetry, which is to say, most literary fiction, endured well into the sixteenth century, and very likely beyond. As one scholar remarks, about the crucial period towards the end of the sixteenth century when opera was in the process of being "invented":

> a poem was conceived as an oral presentation (either sung or recited) for a group of listeners . . .. Even when reciting to oneself it was usual to speak the words aloud. Orality was therefore essential to the process of creation, where the poet moved in a universe that was primarily auditory rather than optical, and where he thought in terms of sound and time rather than architectonic form and space. The poem was apprehended as a tonal realization, whether it was heard in performance or read in private.[23]

What I want first to elicit from these brief historical considerations is that throughout *most* of its career, fictional literature has been a *performance* art: an oral and auditory art. We tend, it appears to me, to think of the whole history of fictional literature, from antiquity to the present, as evolving in two parallel streams: performed literature, which is to say, drama, with the Greek plays as the *fons et origo* of that stream; and read-to-yourself literature, with the Homeric epics as *its* earliest examples. But the truth is quite otherwise. The whole history of fictional literature, until relatively recently, has been *one* stream only: the performance stream. And at some point, not much earlier than the early modern period, the stream diverged into two branches: the performance branch, properly so-called, and the read-to-yourself branch, with the modern novel as its centerpiece.

How should we view this bifurcation? One way to see it is as a drastic ontological break: a drastic metaphysical discontinuity. Before the advent of silent reading, there was but one metaphysics of literature: the work/performance ontology. After the advent of the silently read poem, and the modern novel, there were two: the work/performance and the work – . . .? Aye: there's the rub. How are we to understand the second ontology?

But there is another way. We can see the stream of literature as a continuous one of work/performance ontology. We are encouraged to do so, for one, because fictional literature, *all* fictional literature, has been, for almost *all* of its history, a history of literature as performance, even when the literature has been "read" in private by the solitary reader. For even then he was read to, or read aloud, performed aloud, to himself. Silently read fictional literature, viewed in this perspective, is not discontinuous with its historical predecessors. It is completely continuous with them and with their history. Reading silently, viewed in this way, is not an ontological change from the work/performance ontology. It is just the next logical step, into a performance of a different kind, a silent performance, but clearly recognizable as *performance*. That, at least, is what this monograph is meant to convince you of.

7 Other People's Mail

There can of course be no doubt that the invention of the printing press and of movable type were landmarks in the development of a "reading public." But even that, as is well known, failed to put books in everyone's hands or result in widespread literacy. Books remained expensive commodities until methods of cheap manufacture were developed. And anyone who has ever compared a seventeenth-century book with an eighteenth-century one knows that the former is usually in far better condition because it remains a "hand-made" artifact.

But if the eighteenth century is where we can place the advent of relatively inexpensive, "mass-produced" books, then, I suggest, it is part of the reason, at least, for it also being the century in which the novel as an art form first becomes prominent. For the novel is the quintessentially "private" work of art, to be experienced alone by the silent reader. And for it to become a popular form of art it must be possible for books to be readily obtainable. You can't curl up with a good novel if you don't have the physical object in your possession. A performance makes one written text available to a large number of people. A novel is one on one: it can only be made available to a large number of people if there is a large number of texts in circulation and affordable by those people. (There, were, by the way, "circulating libraries" in the eighteenth century.)

Needless to say, there can be no doubt that silent reading was by this time a fact of life. And if you imagine the social setting of novel-reading you can easily see why it too would be a requirement for the novel's growing popularity. The novel was very much a middle-class mode of entertainment. Its social setting was the family circle: hearth and home. I said, just now, that the novel is the quintessentially private work of art, read in solitary. But it is also part of family life. Imagine the bedlam of a family of readers, all reading to themselves *out loud*!

In a way, then, the novel was *both* a private and a "social" institution. When you read you read to yourself. And your experience of the work was yours alone, whereas at the rhapsode's performance you are one of a company. But also it was frequently a social setting in which you read, as I imagine it: the family circle. Although, obviously, reading alone must also have been a common thing. After all, when there is nobody around to talk to, reading a good novel is a way of entertaining yourself.

In any event, if my armchair history of the fictional literary experience is anywhere near the mark, fictional literature was largely a performing art until relatively recently. Furthermore, if the eighteenth century is indeed the century in which reading novels silently to yourself becomes a major player in the art world, the novel the major non-performance allographic art work, it will not come as a surprise that the first aesthetic theories of the fiction-reading experience, which were advanced in the eighteenth century, were really performance theories, suitably modified to accommodate a silent-reading art.

There is a useful analogy to be drawn between the rise of the novel in the eighteenth century and the invention of opera at the end of the sixteenth.

The most popular opera plot in the early days of the new art form was the Orpheus legend. I think there is an obvious reason for this. People then must have found it difficult, as many people still do, to accept the artistic convention of a drama in which characters sing what we ordinarily speak. As one English critic put it, more than one hundred years after the event, his compatriots found it odd to hear generals singing their commands. But Orpheus *is* a singer, and his story is a story in which his singing plays the major part. So the early audiences to opera were gotten over a rough spot, generals singing their commands, with the aid of a character whose main form of expression, "in real life," was song, not speech.

Now suppose it was the case that the novel, an allographic but non-performance art form, posed a similar problem for its early "audiences" to the one that "generals singing their commands" did for the first audiences of the opera. As the early audiences of opera were bothered more than we are by singing speakers, so the early novel readers may have been bothered, as we are not, by *silent* speakers (and narrators). After all, we consider silent reading of stories the most natural thing in the world. But it must not have always been thus. And in a world where literature was, not so far back, an almost entirely performed art, even when you read to yourself, then, a silent, non-performed story might well have seemed as strange to you as generals singing their commands.

But suppose there was a kind of half-way house between performed literature and silently read, non-performed literature, as there was between spoken drama and sung drama, namely, sung drama with a "real life" singer in the lead role. Would one not suspect that that novelistic half-way house would be particularly popular and in vogue during the period when the novel was in the process of gaining a foothold and gradually acclimatizing people to its special artistic character, namely, as a silently read, non-performance art experience? Well there *is* just such a half-way house, and it had its heyday, *was* most in vogue in the eighteenth century. I have reference to the letter novel, of which Samuel Richardson's *Pamela* and *Clarissa Harlowe* are the two most famous examples.

What is interesting about the letter novel, that is to say, a novel that tells its story in the form of letters by fictional persons is that when you read it you are *performing* it, *even when you are reading it to yourself in silence.* "I read, therefore I perform."

Consider the letter. When Julius Caesar read a letter from his wife, presumably he read it *aloud* to himself. But when Adam Smith read a letter from David Hume, he read it *silently* to himself. He was part of a silent reading culture, as Caesar was not. Of course we sometimes read our letters aloud to our family or friends; but the usual way we read them is the silent way.

Now when I read the play *Hamlet* to myself, silently, I'm not performing, at least in the usual sense of "perform" applied to theatrical works. But what about when I read the novel, *Pamela*, to myself, silently – in the usual way of reading a novel? The perhaps surprising answer I want to suggest is that I *am* performing it. I cannot help but be. With regard to the letter novel, to read is to perform.

When you read a letter from your friend your reading of the letter is a human action, an action which includes, I think, your comprehending its meaning. But when you read one of Pamela's "letters," you are not reading *letters*: you are reading artistic representations of letters. There was no Pamela, and (therefore) there were no letters. Your reading of *these* letters, like your reading of the letter from your friend, is a human action: again, an action that includes understanding their meaning. It is *not*, however, the human action of reading letters. What it is, I suggest, is the human action of performing the part, acting the part of a letter reader, as you would be if you were playing on the stage someone reading a letter silently to herself, with the difference, of course, that the letter you read on stage may very well be a blank piece of paper, for all that it matters, and comprehending the meaning of the letter while reading is not what is going on.

I am not altogether clear about the exact ontology of silent, fictional letter reading, and what I am doing here is entertaining a thought experiment, as it were. It seems odd to say that I am acting myself reading when I read a letter novel. If the letters are to some specified fictional character, then perhaps I am meant to be playing the part of the fictional character reading the letter, Pamela's father or mother, for example. If the recipient is left blank, then I could be understood to be playing the part of a letter reader much like me, except for having access to these letters. Did I find them in my great aunt's attic, tied together in a bundle? (If the novel is *Clarissa*, it would be a pretty thick bundle.)

In any case, whatever the exact nature of performer and performance, a performance seems to me to be what reading a letter novel might be understood as being, although I do not deny that there are other possible alternatives. And the same can be said, I think, for that other popular eighteenth-century novel type, the "journal" or "diary" novel, where the reader plays the part of a journal or diary reader, but, I presume, the idea is much the same. Whoever "I" am, I am not reading a diary or journal. I am reading an artistic representation of one; more exactly, I am acting the part of someone reading a diary or journal, under the hypothesis being entertained here.

Now the point is that, with letter and journal novels, the relation of token to type, and audience to work, might be seen as more clear and unproblematic to an audience that is used to performance literature but not so much to the new, non-performance literary form of the novel, because even though these are novels, they are also, clearly, performed novels. And the performer is not far to seek: it is the reader himself. He is the audience to his own performance, as was Plato when he read the *Iliad* (aloud) to himself, and the amateur pianist, when she played the Beethoven sonatas to herself. He is the audience to his silent performance of reading diary or journal or letter. (It will be seen to follow from this that there are two objects of appreciation here: the literary work *and* the reading performance of it, just as, in a musical performance, there is work appreciation and performance appreciation. This somewhat thorny question will be tackled later on.)

Related to these forms of the novel is the "Call me Ishmael" variety. Here the conceit is not that the reader is perusing letters, or a journal or diary, but listening, presumably, to someone who's "got his ear," perhaps on the streets of New Bedford, and going to tell him his troubles (which in Ishmael's case are considerable). A step removed from the narrator of his own story (in which he plays a principal part, usually) is the Ancient Mariner who is *described as* telling his story by a third party whom some have called the" disembodied narrative voice." (His troubles are not unlike Ishmael's.) But we don't hear the story directly from his lips. We hear it in one long quotation from the lips of the disembodied voice (as we hear the conversation of Socrates and his friends on the last day of his life from the lips of Phaedo). And, finally, as a step away from the quotation narrative, all artifice is put away and the disembodied voice just launches into the story. "The mole had been working very hard all morning, spring-cleaning his little home."

Now one might conjecture that what we have here is a kind of step-by-step initiation into the experience of silently read, non-performance, fictional literature. We go by stages from letters, journals, and other written documents, to hearing spoken narratives by somewhat garrulous strangers, to hearing their stories related verbatim by equally garrulous third parties, to, finally, *just reading the story.* There may be a smidgen of truth in this way of looking at things; but not very much. Here is why.

The step from reading letters and journals and listening to Ishmael tell his story may seem like a small one, but it is not: it is a metaphysical chasm. When you go from Pamela to Ishmael you cross an ontological divide. For when you read Pamela's letters, you are *reading*; but when you "listen" to Ishmael's troubles, you are *not* listening: you are reading as well. And it doesn't matter whether you are reading the story told by Ishmael, reading the story told by the Ancient Mariner and quoted by a disembodied narrator, or simply reading the disembodied narrator's story straight from the horse's mouth. Reading representations of letters and journals is still reading; but reading Ishmael tell his story is not listening to Ishmael.

What I am arguing, then, is that the letter and journal novels provided an easy passage from performed fictional literature, which had so long a reign in the West, if my armchair history and analysis are near the mark, to the new aesthetics of silently read, non-performed literature, of which the novel is the prime exemplar. For in reading the letter or journal novel I am attending a performance of which I am also the performer. I cannot help but be, since in reading even silently, the letter or journal novel, I am acting out the part of someone (never mind who) reading letter or journal.

But when we go beyond this, even to the seeming closely related novel form where I "listen" to a character tell his tale, the "Call me Ishmael" genre, we have crossed a great ontological (and aesthetic) divide to an art form that is not, in any *obvious* way, a performance art. So it requires a new accounting. To that I turn.

8 A Theory of Language

If the first century of the modern novel, which I presume the eighteenth century was, was so close to the tradition of literature, even read-to-yourself literature, as a performing art, it should come as no surprise that the first sustained philosophical attempts to deal with it, where the concept of literal performance fails, are attempts to see it as, so to speak, a performance art in disguise. It may not be *obvious* that the narrative novel, without the artifice of letter or journal, is a performance art; but if you peek around the mask that's what you will find. The argument centers on the famous line from Horace: *Ut pictura poesis*. But what makes the argument is a theory of language: Locke's theory. Without such a theory *Ut pictura poesis* cannot get off the ground. So we must look to Locke's theory of language, very briefly, as it is put forward in Book III of the *Essay Concerning Human Understanding*, before getting on.

Here is what Locke says that is directly relevant to our business:

> Concerning Words also it is farther to be considered. *First*, That they being immediately the Signs of Mens *Ideas*; and, by that means, the Instruments whereby Men communicate their Conceptions, and express to one another those Thoughts and Imaginations, they have within their own Breasts, *there comes by constant use, to be such a Connection between certain Sounds, and the* Ideas *they stand for*, that the Names heard, almost as readily excite certain *Ideas*, as if the Objects themselves, which are apt to produce them, did actually affect the Senses. Which is manifestly so in all obvious sensible Qualities; and in all Substances, that frequently and familiarly occur to us.[24]

To understand what Locke is saying here we must have in hand at least an inkling of how he construes human perception of the external world, while avoiding, as much as possible, involvement in the scholarly disputes over how Locke is to be interpreted in this regard. When I am seeing, say, a green apple, what I am experiencing is an "idea" in my own mind: that idea Locke would say is what I am directly aware of in perception. More accurately, what I am aware of is a "complex" idea, consisting of "simple" ideas such as that of the apple's color, its shape, and so forth. But the cause of my having this complex idea is, of course, an *apple* in my visual field. Thus: "*Our Senses*, conversant about particular sensible Objects, do *convey into the Mind*, several distinct *Perceptions* of things, according to those various ways, wherein those Objects do affect them: and thus we come by those *Ideas*, we have of *Yellow*, *White*, *Heat*, *Cold*, *Soft*, *Hard*, *Bitter*, *Sweet*, and all those which we call sensible qualities, which when I say the senses convey into the mind, I mean, what produces there those *Perceptions*."[25]

Now there is a good deal of dispute among the experts about what exactly Locke's theory of perception is. But for our purposes all that is important is what Locke maintains the relation is *between* what we experience when we perceive the apple and what we experience when we hear or read a description of the apple. In effect, he is saying that it is the *same* experience, at least in certain essential respects. My experience of perceiving the apple consists in my being aware of "apple ideas." And that is also what my experience consists in when I read or hear a description of the apple. As Locke puts it in the passage initially quoted, "the Names heard [or read], almost as readily excite certain *Ideas*, as if the Objects themselves, which are apt to produce them, did actually affect the Senses."

One can well compare the description "green apple," on the Lockean view, to a realistic picture of a green apple. On an old, traditional, and not altogether contemptible theory of what happens when I see such a picture, the story is that the picture presents stimuli to the eye enough like the stimuli produced by a real apple to cause us to "see in" the picture a green apple.[26] What that means is that the stimuli of the picture as well as the stimuli of the object both cause, through excitation of the eye, similar "ideas" of a green apple to be aroused in the mind of the person. It is the experiencing of the idea, whether produced by the apple stimuli or the picture stimuli, that is the experience of perceiving the apple in reality or "seeing in" the picture a green apple. Pictures, in other words, *like verbal descriptions*, "almost as readily excite certain *Ideas*, as if the Objects themselves, which are apt to produce them, did actually affect the Senses."

Of course there is one great difference between pictures (of the kind I am speaking of) and words. To stick to our example, a picture of a green apple will cause *anyone* to have aroused in his or her mind the idea of a green apple and thus "see in" the picture a green apple. But the words "green apple" do this by a linguistic convention. As Locke says, it is only because "*there comes by constant use*, to be such a *Connexion between certain Sounds* [or written inscriptions], and the Ideas they stand for . . .," that words, spoken or written, have this power to arouse the correspondent ideas in the hearer's or reader's mind. Once, however, "such *a*

Connexion" is made, then the picture and the phrase, on the Lockean understanding of language, function in much the same way. To be sure by different causal pathways, they both produce the same idea in the mind that the subject would have had if she had seen the green apple. So, quite literally, a description, on the Lockean model of language and perception, *is* a picture: picture and description are functionally equivalent. You are having "close to" the same experience, on the Lockean model, whether you are seeing a green apple, seeing a picture of a green apple, or hearing the words "green apple" (assuming of course that you understand English).

The Lockean does not want to say that your experience of seeing a green apple is indistinguishable from seeing a picture of one or hearing the words "green apple" enunciated. A person for whom that was the case would be a victim of illusion or hallucination. But certainly what Locke was committed to is that the three experiences are of a kind. Or, to put it another way, on this view the experience of hearing or reading descriptions, is more like that of seeing pictures than one might ordinarily have thought, and, therefore, far more like seeing (or otherwise sensing) the depicted things than one might ordinarily have thought. And, furthermore, I suggest that this model of perception and language was the foundation on which the eighteenth-century philosophers of art built their theory of read literature. That theory I now want to look at, with these background remarks in mind.

9 Productions in the Mind

Philosophers' and other theorists' remarks on fictional literature, in the eighteenth century, are usually remarks about "poetry." And it is a commonplace of the period that poetry is an "imitative" art, like painting and sculpture. But, clearly, it cannot be imitative in exactly the same way in which painting and sculpture can. Paintings and statues resemble, are "imitative" of the objects depicted. But surely *words* are not that. As Edmund Burke put the point, in his widely admired *Philosophical Enquiry into the Origin of Our Ideas of the Sublime and Beautiful* (1757), "Nothing is an imitation further than as it resembles some other thing; and words undoubtedly have no sort of resemblance to the ideas for which they stand."[27] Or, again, as Alexander Gerard, another popular writer of the period said of "language or artificial signs," "these bear no resemblance to the things signified by them."[28]

Of course those who *did* think read poetry or literature an imitative art knew full well that words or sentences don't look like their objects. What they meant, aided and abetted by Locke's theory of perception and language, is that the conscious states aroused by words – by word-descriptions – are significantly like the conscious states one would be in if one were perceiving the objects, characters, and situations those words describe.

To get an idea of what this claim looks like one can turn, for example, to Joseph Addison's *Spectator* papers that he called "On the Pleasures of the Imagination" (1711–1712). In the sixth of these papers, he initiates a discussion of the pleasure we take in literary description in this wise: "Here, therefore, we must inquire after a new principle of pleasure, which is nothing else but the action of the mind, which compares the ideas that arise from words with the ideas that arise from the objects themselves . . .."[29] It seems quite clear from this passage that Addison is thinking along more or less Lockean lines, as regards both perception and language, in his treatment of literary discourse. The experience of perception is thought of as the experience of "ideas that arise from the objects themselves," and understanding, of descriptive language, at least, as the experiencing of "ideas that arise from words," while the adequacy or accuracy of description is cashed out in terms of how closely "the ideas that arise from words" *resemble* "the ideas that arise from the objects themselves." Poetry or literature, then, is an "imitative" art in so far as its language causes to arise in us ideas of the kind we would experience if we were actually perceiving the objects, characters, and events of which the language speaks.

Addison had a prominent and distinguished follower, in this regard, in Thomas Reid, who, in his lectures to his advanced students at the University of Glasgow, beginning in 1764, advocated a similar view of literary prose, although already expressed in distinctly Reidian perceptual language. Thus we find in one of his lecture notes: "Description of Passions and Affections the chief Beauty in Poetry. Poetical Description is painting to the Imagination by Describing the Natural Signs and concomitants of those things illustrating them by [figures] Metaphors Similitudes &c."[30]

That Reid knew Addison's theory of literary language is all but certain, as he states specifically, in the same lecture notes, that "The Subject," which is to say, the whole subject of the fine arts, or arts of taste, "has been handled by many late Writers of Taste and Judgment. By Adison [*sic*] in his Papers on the Pleasures of Imagination . . .," among numerous others named.[31] But even in the very brief statement of the Addisonian literary theory, quoted above, Reid has already translated it into the terms of his own theory of perception and expression.

The passage can be glossed somewhat along the following lines. Reid thought that the major subject of the fine arts is the expression of the human emotions. Human beings express their emotions in various forms of behavior, both bodily and vocal, that are "Natural Signs" of those emotions. The art of painting pictures those "Natural Signs" to our sight in the visual depiction of human beings in expressive attitudes. And literary fiction "pictures" those "Natural Signs" to the "Imagination" through words by exciting in it the mental images of human beings in expressive attitudes. Although the concept of "Natural Signs," and the emphasis on emotive expression as the subject of the fine arts is distinctly Reid's, the bare outline of the theory is along the lines of Addison, by Locke, even though, as is well known, Reid's theory of perception departed from Locke's in various crucial ways. But the bottom line is, for both Addison *and* Reid (to quote Reid again): "Poetical Description is painting to the Imagination . . .."

That the British were not the only ones thinking along these lines, at the time, can be amply demonstrated by turning to the Continental tradition for a moment: in particular, to Alexander Baumgarten, who, as is well known, gave us the word "aesthetic" as the name of our discipline. For Baumgarten too, while coming from the rationalist, Cartesian/Leibnizian tradition, not the tradition of Lockean empiricism, construed the silent reading of literary fiction, or at least of poetry, as a form of inner sense perception, which was why, of course, it was part of what he called the "science" of "aesthetics."

There is no need to delve too deeply into Baumgarten's semi-deductive mode of exposition, in the *Reflections on Poetry* (of 1735), the work where the word "aesthetics" was first coined. It will suffice for us to run quickly through some of his "definitions" to get a good idea of what he was about.

"By **sensate representations**," Baumgarten writes, "we mean representations received through the lower part of the cognitive faculty," which is to say, the *perceptual* faculty.[32] "By **sensate discourse**," he continues, "we mean discourse involving sensate representations,"[33] and "By **perfect sensate discourse** we mean discourse whose various parts are directed toward the apprehension of sensate representations . . .."[34] Thus "A sensate discourse will be the more perfect the more its parts favor the awakening of sensate representations"; and "By **poem** we mean a perfect sensate discourse . . .."[35] Finally, following Leibniz, and the Cartesian terminology of clear and distinct ideas, Baumgarten characterizes "poetic representations" as "clear but confused."[36]

Without going any further into Baumgarten's historically crucial discussion of poetry, we can make the general observations, for present purposes, that, like Addison and Reid, he must be construing the experience of the poetic literary work as a kind of inner sense perception. For assuming that "sensate representations" are mental representations given us in external perception, we clearly should construe the claim that "sensate discourse" involves "the awakening of sensate representations" as meaning that sensate discourse, of which poetic discourse is the prime example, arouses in the mind "sensate representations," which is to say, mental images of sensible objects, for some "inner sense" to perceive. Nor does Baumgarten leave this conclusion unstated. He writes: "the representation of a picture is very similar to the sense idea to be depicted, and this is poetic . . .. Therefore, a poem and a picture are similar . . .," or, in a word, "*Poetry is like a picture*."[37]

Thus, although arrived at in very different ways, the conclusions of Baumgarten, Addison, and Reid are basically the same. The experience of poetry, and, if one dares to generalize, silently read fictional narrative *tout court*, is a *perceptual* experience, albeit an experience of an inner perception, principally, if the examples that all three provide are to be credited, an experience largely of inner *visual* perception.

But what exactly would we perceive if we were present at the events narrated, say, by *Tom Jones*, according to the theories of Addison, Reid, and perhaps even Baumgarten, outlined above? When I read Gibbon's *Decline and Fall*, on the Lockean model, I will have excited in me by at least *some* of the author's prose – the "descriptive," not the "interpretive" – ideas very like the ones I would have had excited in me had I been an eye-witness to the historical events described (although what I took the events to be that I was observing would depend, of course, on the nature and extent of my historical perspective). *Tom Jones*, however, is not history; it is fiction. The events recounted therein never took place; there never was a Tom Jones, a Mr. Allworthy, a Mr. Western, and the rest.

Given the Lockean model of perception and language, and perhaps that of Baumgarten as well, given the eighteenth-century context, I think the most natural way of representing what was being said is to say that when I read *Tom Jones* the language excites in me ideas very like those I would have had excited in me had I been at a performance of *Tom Jones*. What kind of performance? Obviously a dramatic one: a performance of a play. Nor do I think it reading something into eighteenth-century thought to put things this way. The dramatic image occurs frequently. I adduce an example, indeed, from Reid himself, in his *Essays on the Intellectual Powers of Man* (1785). I doubt I would have to look very hard for another. Reid writes of the *Iliad*: "When we consider the things presented to our mind in the 'Iliad' without regard to the poet, the grandeur is properly in Hector and Achilles, and the other great personages, human and divine, *brought upon the stage*."[38] The Lockean, Addisonian picture of the reading experience, in poetic or prose fiction is, I suggest, the experience of "seeing" (and "hearing") in the imagination, in the mind's eye, a dramatic representation: a theatrical production in the mind. The novelist is the playwright, the novel the script. The director is you.

That this is the way many people might still describe their experience of silently read fiction I strongly suspect. Ludwig Wittgenstein, for example, gave a very vivid presentation of it in the collection of his "sayings" known as the *Zettel*, most of which the editors date as having been written between 1945 and 1948.[39] Whether it is a view he himself adhered to at this time or whether it is a view presented to be refuted I am in no position even to guess, not myself being a student of the Wittgensteinian corpus (although even I can see that the underlying ideas about language and meaning seem more *Tractatus*-like than anything else).

In any event, Wittgenstein says in the *Zettel*, of how he (or someone?) reads a story: "I . . . have impressions, see pictures in my mind's eye, etc. I make the story pass before me like pictures, like a cartoon story."[40] He then adds the parenthetical caveat: "Of course I don't mean by this that every sentence summons up one or more visual images, and that that is, say, the purpose of a sentence."[41] And the next "Zettel" reads: "'Sentences serve to describe how things are,' we think. The sentence as a *picture*."[42]

Again, I cannot venture an opinion about whether this is a view of fictional language and the fictional experience (in the literary sense) that Wittgenstein ever held, or whether it is proposed in the *Zettel* merely as a position important enough, and live enough to be considered and refuted. That it was during Wittgenstein's lifetime, and still is, a widely held view, at least among lay readers, of the way literary fiction presents itself in silent reading, I have little doubt. And the way Wittgenstein outlines the view, although typically Wittgensteinian in its teasing manner, is a very palpable version of the Locke/Addison package, which consists, in the *Zettel*, in three propositions, all, it is clear, consistent with the views of Locke and Addison I have been outlining above. First, in reading literary fiction silently to one's self, the story passes before one's mind's eye like a series of pictures. Second, this does not imply that *all* sentences function the way fictional picture-producing sentences do: a limit on the image-evoking function of language that I am sure Locke not only would have but did (at least implicitly) endorse. And, finally, as Wittgenstein puts it, the fictional sentence is as a picture. For, as I have argued above, on the Lockean view, drawn to its logical conclusion, descriptive words and sentences are, in something close to a literal sense, pictorial, at least if a certain analysis of what it means to be a pictorial image is accepted as an approximation of the truth.[43]

As I have said, it seems to me no surprise that what I guess is the first philosophical theory of literary fiction as a silently read art form should tend to present it as a silent *performance*. For if I am right in my previous historical speculations, literary fiction was mainly a performing art for most of its history, up to the eighteenth century, even when one read it to oneself. Small wonder, then, that the notion of performance should dominate thinking about silently read fiction. It must have been difficult to think about it in any other terms. It is not, I believe, just that the image of characters in a novel or narrative poem stepping onto a stage of the mind was a readily available and appropriate metaphor. Given the Lockean theory of perception and language, it was much more than that. It was a theory in its own right of the read-in-silence fictional experience. And at its core, I believe, *it was absolutely right*. It is the theory, indeed, that I intend to defend in this book.

However, the performance theory of silently read fiction, as formulated by Addison and other explicit or implicit Lockeans, was also profoundly mistaken. For it had as its linguistic foundation a profoundly mistaken theory. And there were those in the eighteenth century who knew this already full well. So before I try to defend my own version of reading as performance I had better first examine the eighteenth-century critique of the Addisonian version, which emanates principally from Burke.

10 The Effect of Words

Part V of Burke's *Philosophical Enquiry* is devoted to the nature of poetry, in light of the claim of his contemporaries that poetry, for which I read fictional narrative, is an "imitative" art. It is also a trenchant critique of the Lockean take on language.

To begin at the beginning, Burke writes in Section I of Part V, "Of Words,"

> Natural objects affect us, by the laws of that connexion, which Providence has established between certain motions and configurations of bodies, and certain consequent feelings [i.e. ideas] of our minds. Painting affects in the same manner, but with the superadded pleasure of imitation . . . .. But as to words; they seem to me to affect us in a manner very different from that in which we are affected by natural objects, or by painting . . ..[44]

Of course no Lockean would disagree with this very general statement of the distinction between words, and pictures or perceptions. If you mean by the "manner" in which words "affect" one the causal process by which they do the business, then in very important respects, the Lockean would agree, words indeed "affect us in a manner very different from that in which we are affected by natural objects, or by painting . . .." But if you mean by the "manner" in which words "affect" one the *result* of the causal machinery, then what the Lockean is saying is that this effect, the conscious state, is importantly the same whether the business is done by a natural object, or by a painting, or by "words."

A word about "words." It hardly needs stating that it makes little sense to include in what I have been calling the Lockean model of language such words as "not," "therefore," "or," and the like. Furthermore, of what Burke calls "compound abstracts, such as virtue, honour, persuasion, docility," he avers that "whatever power they may have on the passions, they do not derive it from any representation raised in the mind of the things for which they stand."[45] Thus there are many words, both for the Lockean and for his critics, that are simply not amenable to an image-arousal model. If the Lockean model has any plausibility at all it must be for words other than these. For Burke the viable candidates are what he calls "aggregate words," which "are such as represent many simple ideas *united by* nature to form some one determinate composition, as man, house, tree, castle, &c.," and "simple abstract words," which "stand for one simple idea of such composition and no more; as red, blue, round, square, and the like."[46]

To cut through the verbiage, I shall simply say that what the Lockean model is meant to apply to, in the Addisonian theory of read literature, and what I am concerned with in this particular place, is descriptive language as it is used in literary narrative fiction. This, in any event, is what Burke is talking about.

Another important point can be gleaned from the way Burke expresses his conviction that the "compound abstracts" do not fit the Lockean linguistic model. They do not derive whatever emotive effect they may have "from any representation raised in the mind of the things for which they stand." The point is that Burke clearly construes Locke's theory of perception as some kind of "image" theory: that in perception our conscious states are "images" of things in the external world. And if you want to plead the case that a representation need not be construed as an image or resemblance, Burke makes it very plain in Section IV, "The Effect of Words," where his attack on the Lockean model of language is launched, that images or resemblances are precisely what he is talking about. For he says both of simple abstracts and aggregates, which are at least *prima facie* candidates for the Lockean model, "But I am of opinion that the most general effect even of these words, does not arise from their forming pictures of the several things they would represent in the imagination, because on a very diligent examination of my own mind, and getting others to consider theirs, I do not find that one in twenty times any such picture is formed, and when it is, there is most commonly a particular effort of the imagination for that purpose."[47]

Now I have very carefully avoided expressing either Locke's theory of perception or his theory of language in terms of images or pictures. I have merely referred to the conscious states that we have in perceiving and the perception-like conscious states that, on the Lockean model, descriptive language is supposed to arouse. I have done so for two reasons. First, I do not want my argument to become involved with the disputed interpretational question of whether Locke thought any of our perceptions "resemble," or are "images" or "pictures" of their objects, although I am much inclined to hold, with Michael Ayers, that he did. "Despite the relative unpopularity of an affirmative answer, the grounds for holding him an imagist are conclusive."[48]

My second reason, the more important one, is that I do not want the question of whether the Addisonian theory of read fictional narrative is true to turn on whether an imagist theory of perception is true. Or, rather, I want to argue that it is *not* true, whatever one's theory of perception is.

For these reasons I have expressed the Lockean theory as simply being that descriptions arouse in us conscious states significantly like the conscious states aroused in perception of the objects, characters, and states of affairs described, and the Addisonian theory of read narrative fiction as holding that literary narratives arouse in us conscious states significantly like the ones aroused in us in perceiving staged performances of them. I have avoided characterizing those conscious states in Lockean or any other theoretical terms. We all know by direct acquaintance what they are, and that is enough.

As we get on with Burke's critique of the Addisonian take on read fiction, then, we must bear in mind that its underlying assumption is an imagist one: its target is an imagist model of linguistic description founded upon an imagist theory of perception. But I will take its target to be, as well, simply a theory of linguistic and literary description to the effect that descriptions in general, and literary ones in particular, arouse in us conscious states significantly like those aroused by perception of the objects, characters, events, and states of affairs so described. With that caveat in place, we can get on with it.

We have seen that Burke begins his critique of the Lockean linguistic model by, in effect, appealing to introspection: his and his readers'. The claim is that if you examine what your conscious states are while reading descriptions, you will find that they simply do not contain images or pictures of the things described. Furthermore, he then adds, "Indeed it is impossible in the rapidity and quick succession of words in conversation, to have ideas both of the sound of the word, and of the thing represented . . .."[49] In general terms, then, Burke's argument is that introspection reveals no perception-like states of consciousness when we read or listen to descriptions; and common sense tells us that the rapid flow of language would not allow enough time for such states to be aroused anyway. The Lockean linguistic model stands up neither to experience nor to reason.

It is an easy step from here – from the general critique of the Lockean linguistic model – to the rejection of the Addisonian theory of read literature, which relies on the Lockean model for its *modus operandi*. For what language in general cannot do, literary description and narrative, in particular, cannot do either.

> In short, it is not only of those ideas which are commonly called abstract and of which no image at all *can* be formed, but even of particular real beings, that we converse without having any idea of them excited in the imagination; as will certainly appear on a diligent examination of our own minds. Indeed, so little does poetry depend for its effect on the power of raising sensible images, that I am convinced it would lose a very considerable part of its energy if this were the necessary result of all description.[50]

It is no part of my purpose here to launch an overall critique of Locke's philosophy of language. It has been roundly criticized by contemporary writers for various of its features, and defended, at least in part, by Michael Ayers on the grounds that a normative account has been mistaken for a descriptive one.[51] But that is not my business. Rather, I am concerned with only one aspect of it, its apparently imagist strain, and the imagist theory of silently read narrative fiction – the Addisonian theory – for which it provided the foundation. For I think Burke is right on the mark in his criticism of Addisonian "imagism" as an account of read literature and have advanced similar criticism on another occasion myself.[52]

What further needs to be said is that we remind ourselves of exactly how we are taking the imagist account of language and silently read literature. There is no need to place heavy emphasis on the notion that language, literary or not, raises in us mental pictures. The more general claim is that it produces experiences significantly like the experiences one would have if confronted in perception with the objects, characters, and events described by language. That claim makes no assumptions about what analysis of perception is understood. And, I suggest, Burke's criticism of the Addisonian theory of silently read literature, in its original, Addisonian version, that is to say, the imagist version, is good against any other account of silently read narrative fiction that interprets the reading experience as a more or less visual perceptual experience. Introspection and common sense are as much against that general form of the theory as they are against the Addisonian, imagistic version.

But one part of Burke's critique we can certainly put aside. It is the part hinted at by his statement, quoted above, that if literary description *were* imagistic, then "it would lose a very considerable part of its energy . . .." For what Burke is alluding to here is his own theory of read literature, which is, essentially, that the major intended, and appropriate effect of literary language is an emotional effect. As he states the view:

> The truth is, all verbal description, merely as naked description, though never so exact, conveys so poor and insufficient an idea of the thing described, that it could scarcely have the smallest effect, if the speaker did not call in to his aid those modes of speech that mark a strong and lively feeling in himself. Then, by the contagion of our passions, we catch a fire already kindled in another, which probably might never have been struck out by the object described. Words, by strongly conveying the passions, by those means which we have already mentioned, fully compensate for their weakness in other respects.[53]

The gist of what Burke is arguing, then, seems to be this. It is the proper role of literary language, not to raise images but to arouse the passions in readers. (That he is talking about spoken language in the passage quoted above is immaterial.) And if literary language *did* – which it does not – have the power to raise images, that in fact, would interfere with its primary artistic function of emotive arousal. For the raising of images is supposed to substitute for perceiving itself, on the Addisonian model; and the emotive "fire," Burke avers, "might never have been struck out by the object described," that is, by seeing it.[54] Emotive, not descriptive language is what does the job.

What Burke is suggesting here is a proto-version of what has come to be called an expression theory of art. It is, more precisely, a self-expression theory, which has it that the primary function of literary language is to arouse emotions in the reader (or listener) that are first felt by the author and then, by "contagion," subsequently felt by his audience.

Now I say that this "positive" aspect of Burke's critique should be put aside – but not because I think it is false that read literature can, as an important part of its artistic effect, arouse emotions in readers. But I neither think that it is the only function of description, nor do I think the self-expression theory and its accompanying contagion theory have anything to do with this. As well, I *do* think a major role of descriptive literary language is *descriptive*. (What else?) It is the Addisonian version of description that, I think, Burke is perfectly right in rejecting.

11 A Musical Interlude

It does not sound odd to suggest that musical scores and dramatic texts are logically similar artifacts. From each a performance is derived; and the customary way of experiencing each is through the performance so derived.

So far I have tried to show that for a large part of its history, literary fiction, even when not in the form of performed drama, was *also* a performing art, although we do not think of it that way today. For until the advent of silent reading, and the spread of literacy, which are relatively recent phenomena, even "reading to oneself" was a performance: either a performance by oneself, if one read aloud to oneself, or a "being read to" performance, if one was read to by a servant or a slave.[55]

I argued as well that when silent reading did become a common way to experience narrative fiction, the first aesthetic "theory" of silent reading, the Addisonian one, represented the experience of reading as an inner, mental performance in the mind's eye, as it were: a theatrical production in the mind. And I concluded that this theory, following Burke, simply will not wash because it is based on a faulty view of descriptive language: the Lockean view, broadly conceived, that descriptions stimulate conscious experiences significantly like perceptual experiences, that is to say, experiences of actually perceiving the characters, objects, and events described.

What I would like to do now is to examine briefly the musical score, in light of the conclusions we have so far reached about the experience of a silently read fictional text. I think it has something relevant and important to teach us.

I begin with two definitions. *Score*: "The notation of a work, especially one for ensemble, presented in such a way that simultaneous moments in all voices or parts are aligned vertically." *Score-reading*: "The internal realization of the sound of a work by means of simply reading the score . . .."[56]

What we learn from these two definitions is that because, in the modern score at least, the vertical alignment of notes coincides with the temporal occurrence of sounds and the simultaneous movements of the voices or instrumental parts, one can, if one is a good enough and talented enough musician, internally realize "the sound of a work by means of simply reading the score." In other words, the musical score and its reader conform precisely to the Addisonian model of silently read narrative fiction. One *can* silently read a musical score and, through the silent reading, "hear" in one's mind the musical work: a realization of the sound of the work. One can "hear" a production in the mind.

But before we get on with this an important caveat must be entered. Reading novels is the customary way of experiencing them, and reading plays is certainly not that unusual. Reading scores, however, and realizing the sounds of musical works in one's mind is decidedly *not* the customary way of experiencing music nor is it anything but *very unusual*. Indeed, the ability to read scores and thereby to successfully experience musical works is part of the aura that surrounds only the most gifted, the account of Beethoven "reading" the scores of Handel's and Schubert's works on his deathbed being a case in point. Of course I am not suggesting that one need be a musical genius to accomplish the feat. Nevertheless, you need to have a musical mind and musical training far beyond even that of most accomplished professional musicians. It is, in other words, a feat of considerable mental power, considerably exceeding that of the average and even above-average musician, *a fortiori*, beyond that of the most avid and devoted music-lover. Yet, I suggest, we can learn from the phenomenon, rare though it is, something about the far more mundane experience of reading to oneself a novel or play.

Of course the analogy between text-reading and score-reading should not be over-drawn, and the gap between the ability to do the former as opposed to the latter underestimated. Nor should the distinction between a reading art, like the novel, and a performing art, like music, be obliterated in the process of being blurred. And *a propos* of this caveat, it is appropriate to call attention to one of the more bizarre suggestions, in this regard, of Theodor Adorno's, where he essentially seems to claim that listening to music could, and indeed *should* fall by the wayside in more enlightened times, as has the necessity of reading aloud to oneself. Adorno writes:

> The need to see something which is essentially a creation of the mind as mediated through its sensuous representation, and then not to grasp and comprehend these representations themselves by means of the mind, is infantile. Just as today it's only old-fashioned country people who read aloud in order to read at all, and just as it's still the case that only the rudimentary movement of the lips is left over when reading from the prayer book, so once it could easily have been the case with music. There is no reason at all to consider the sensuous sound to music to be more essential for music than the sensuous sound of words is for language.[57]

Now aside from the fact that Adorno seems to be unaware of *why* reading aloud to oneself was necessary, and no longer is – it was never "infantile" – the idea that hearing music is not essential for reading music in score surely is flat out false: the latter is parasitic on the former, whereas hearing and speaking a language are not parasitic on silently reading it to oneself, witness the fact that the congenitally deaf can learn to read a linguistic text (although with great difficulty, and imperfectly) whereas they clearly could not learn to read a musical score at all. How could someone born deaf "experience" a Mozart concerto by reading the score (or any other way)? That can only be done by listening to music and learning its notation. Beethoven could do it because he once could hear.

A more charitable interpretation of what Adorno is suggesting here might be this. Just as every child learns to read by first reading aloud, and then ceasing to read aloud after silent reading has been mastered, so, too, in a better, more musically enlightened world, we all would learn to read scores by first listening to or playing music, and then, after mastering the skill of silent score-reading, divest ourselves of the useless and "infantile" habit of music-listening and playing, as we now do the useless and infantile habit of reading aloud or moving our lips, as we did when children. The first obvious problem, of course, with this weaker form of the proposal, is that even if silently reading scores were preferable to normal music-listening, few of us, as I have remarked above, could ever learn to do it, anyway. The vast majority of music-lovers cannot experience music in any other way than by listening to it, whereas every normal human being can learn to read silently.

In addition to this obvious objection, a culture of music-lovers who experienced music solely by silently reading scores would have a musical art-form that simply is not ours. Ours is a *performing* art-form, and performing artists are an essential part of it, their performances works of art in their own right (and more of that anon).

Adorno's idea of music-listening withering away and giving over to score-reading, if that is what the suggestion really is, is not only an impossible dream but an impossible nightmare. And one suspects it might be a response to the oft-repeated charge against the atonal serialism of Schoenberg, Berg, and Webern, which he championed, that it was unlistenable "music for the eyes," with musical structures that could be seen but not heard. Be that as it may, it is not being argued on these pages that score-reading and novel-reading are *identical*; only that the former can provide for us a useful, illuminating analogy for the latter. And it is surely *not* my intention, as it apparently was Adorno's, to transform a performing art into a reading art. So with his bizarre suggestion out of the way, and with the caveat entered that the silent reading of scores is an *analogy*, and an analogy *only* to the silent reading of fiction, let us get on with the task of drawing the analogy more fully.

I begin with the obvious. First, unless you have heard music performed, there is no way you can learn to realize the sounds of music in your mind by reading scores. Second, when someone does succeed in realizing the sounds of a musical work in his head, what he is "hearing" in his head is a particular performance of the music. Third, what he is hearing is *his* performance of the work: either in the sense of hearing the work performed in the manner of a performance he has previously heard, or, executing in his head, his own performance according to his own performance style. But in either case what I want to emphasize is that in reading a score for the purpose of realizing the work in his head, the score-reader is, in effect, performing the work. Score-reading is "silent performance" under the direction of the reader.

A word now is in order concerning the vexed concept of interpretation. I will return to this concept again later on. But something at least must be said about it here.

Two of the most common uses of the word "interpretation" are in reference to works of art. We call what critics say about the meaning and significance of art works interpretations of them, and we call performances interpretations of them. Thus, we contrast A. C. Bradley's Hegelian interpretation of *Hamlet* with Ernest Jones' Freudian interpretation; and we contrast Schnabel's Romantic interpretations of the Beethoven piano sonatas with Brendel's rather more precise and laid back ones.

But, of course, these two uses of the term "interpretation" are closely related. To begin with, contrary to what some believe, it is my view that the term is applied univocally to, for example, A. C. Bradley's written interpretations of Shakespeare's plays and Schnabel's performances of Beethoven's piano sonatas. They are all literally, and in the same sense, interpretations, the difference being that Bradley's book on Shakespeare's plays *tells* you his interpretations, whereas Schnabel's performances of Beethoven *show* you his interpretations.[58] Nor am I alone in thinking this is so, even though there are those who disagree. "Kivy is right: telling how something goes is not the same as showing how it goes. He is also right in saying that the term 'interpretation' can be applied in both cases."[59]

Furthermore, where performances achieve a significant level of sophistication, the performer has an interpretation, a notion of how the music goes, "what makes it tick," that precedes and informs her performance-interpretation. And even if she cannot articulate it verbally, the way Bradley can his interpretations of Shakespeare, musicians generally being non-verbal people, it remains a "telling," rather than a "showing" inter-pretation: it can, in principle, be articulated by someone who knows the interpretation and has the words.[60]

Now the reason the above remarks on interpretation are so important in the present context is that anyone who is capable of realizing a musical work in her head by reading a score is a musician – probably a composer or performer or both – at the very highest level of musical accomplish-ment with a musical mind of fairly impressive dimensions. And such an individual would, without a doubt, have an interpretation, a view of how the music goes, what makes it tick, that would inform her reading of the score. In other words, the performance in the reader's head will be an interpretation in its own right, as performances at any significant level of sophistication are interpretations. And it will be a performance informed by an interpretation, informed by a worked out view of how the music goes, what makes the music tick.

In this, as in other respects, the reading of a score will be in sharp con-trast with the reading of a literary text: a novel, or a narrative poem. For whereas the reading of scores is the exclusive province of experts, the reading of novels and poems is widespread and open not merely to experts but to a large audience of lay persons who need have no literary expertise at all, merely the necessary level of education and sophistication neces-sary for the understanding of whatever fictional narrative is in question. Dentists and accountants, plumbers and carpenters, pilots and bus drivers, lawyers and store keepers, can all read the novels of Dickens. They cannot read the scores of Beethoven's symphonies, although they can, of course, enjoy performances of them at orchestral concerts.

One reason for this disparity between reading novels and reading musical scores is, of course, the obvious fact that reading our own lan-guage seems a "natural" accomplishment, language a basic fact of our lives as human beings, whereas reading music seems far from "natural," and is, indeed, an accomplishment reserved only for the very few cultures that have ever developed musical notations. However, there is, indeed, one thing that stands out sharply in the contrast between reading a score silently to oneself and reading a novel. If the score is of a polyphonic com-position, which is to say, goes beyond the notation of simply a single melody, the composition must sound "in the head" in many "voices" simultaneously: four, for example, in a string quartet, many more in a symphony. Whereas a novel-reading sounds one voice only, at a time, even though it may sometimes be a different voice from that of the storyteller: which is to say, one of the characters in direct quotation.

Thus, apart from the difficulty the average person might have hearing music "in the head," even a single melody, as compared to hearing speech, the sheer complexity of contrapuntal texture is something that few musical minds can realize "in the head," even those of devoted music-listeners and accomplished musicians, let alone the lay person and casual listener. The difficulty then is not only that "speech is speech" and "music is music," with all that implies for the silent reading phenomenon. It is also the multi-layered structure of polyphonic music in the West that the musical score evolved to notate.

An added difficulty, to revert to a point already made, is that all readers of musical scores must have highly sophisticated interpretations of the works they "perform" in their heads, and few readers of literary texts will. But, as I shall argue later on, all readers of literary texts – of novels, poems, and stories – must have *some* interpretation or other of what they read. And as they become more sophisticated readers, they may well avail themselves of the professional literary critics to augment and revise their interpretations. (I will return to this vital point later on as well.)

The reading of musical scores, then, in spite of glaring disparities, comes closer than any other reading experience to the Addisonian theory of silently read narrative fiction. Indeed, one might say that it completely conforms. For those few who are capable of the feat, the musical score produces in the reader's mind an experience in truth *significantly like* the perceptual experience of listening to a sonic performance of the work. Musical notation, then, in the modern score, is Locke's theory of language in the flesh. Does *literary* experience come close to this?

What immediately comes to mind is the dramatic text or script. For it is common sense to think that the script is to the performance of the play as the score is to the performance of the symphony. Why, then, shouldn't it be the case that the reader of the script *sees* a performance of the play in his head as the reader of the score "hears" music? And if the reply is that most readers of plays just don't have the power of imagination to see a play in the mind's eye, the obvious response is that, as we have already granted, most music-lovers, even the trained musicians among them, don't have the power of musical imagination to hear a symphony in the mind's ear. I may not be able to bring before my mind a stage production in all its visual and auditory detail when I read a play. But does that imply that Mike Nichols can't?

It would be foolish to think that people do not vary as regards their abilities to imaginatively visualize silently read dramatic texts; and it might very well be that talented directors of plays and movies greatly exceed the rest of us in this department. Be that as it may, there *is* a difference in kind between the role the visual imagination may play in the reading of scripts and the role of the aural imagination in the reading of scores.

Briefly put, modern musical scores – let us say from the beginning of the eighteenth century – determine all of those parameters necessary for realizing a performance in a manner that enables a proficient score-reader to realize a performance in her head. But a script or dramatic text does not do that. Why one does it, and the other does not, obviously has to do with a number of things. It has to do with the fact that experiencing a musical performance is a matter of one sense modality, whereas a dramatic performance is a matter of two. It has to do with the fact that musical notation and written language are very different kinds of symbol systems.[61] And of course it has to do with how different the experience of reading a linguistic text is from reading a musical one.

That little being said, I will take the occasion to confess that I do not myself understand exactly why there is this difference between score-reading and text-reading. All I can say is that we are the kinds of beings, and those are the kinds of symbol systems, such that some few of us can realize a musical performance in our heads, and none of us, no matter how gifted, can realize the performance of a play in our heads by reading a script. Or to put it another way, the criterion of ultimate, complete success in reading a musical score is realizing a musical performance in the head, whereas the criterion of ultimate, complete success in reading a script is thoroughly understanding it. Those are the facts. That is all.

We cannot conclude, then, even though dramatic texts bear a direct analogy to musical scores, that the analogy extends to silent reading. In particular, the analogy does not suggest that as silent readings of scores realize musical performances in the head, silent readings of dramatic texts realize dramatic productions in the head. There the analogy does not hold. And, *a fortiori*, the analogy does not hold, in that respect, to silent readings of novels. For the novel, by hypothesis, is not a performing art at all, at least in any obvious sense. (Whether it is in any *unobvious* sense remains to be seen.)

Now from what has so far been said about the silent reading of musical scores, it may well be surmised that I think we can learn nothing about the silent reading of plays, or, even more apparently, the silent reading of novels and narrative poems, by examining the phenomenon of silent score-reading. But that is not so; and what we can learn we will discover by and by.

12 Telling Stories

Seeing a movie, seeing a play, reading a novel: they certainly seem to be very different experiences indeed. Most of us, I dare say, would tend to think that experiencing a movie showing and experiencing a play performance are far more similar to one another than either is to novel-reading. What of interest, however, might the three have in common? One obvious answer to this question – and I think a true answer – is that in all three cases we are being told a story, albeit in strikingly diverse ways. As Gregory Currie puts the point I am making, in his book, *The Nature of Fiction*: "The difference between visual and nonvisual fiction lies only in the manner of telling, as that manner is dictated by the medium itself."[62]

There is a great deal in Currie's account of narrative fiction with which I disagree, and there is a great deal that is not relevant to my project here. But the idea of plays, movies, and novels as instances of story telling, obvious though it may be, it seems to me has something of importance to tell us about novel-reading in a not so obvious way. So I want to spend a little time now discussing Currie's proposal and its relevance.

Here, in his own words, is a fuller statement of Currie's view:

> Reading the novel, we make believe that the fictional author is presenting us with information he knows to be true. He is presenting that information verbally. And in the play or film it is similarly make-believe that the fictional author is also presenting us with information he knows to be true. The difference is in the mode of presentation of the information. Imagine the ways in which a storyteller might tell his story. He might describe the events in words. But instead (or in addition) he might act out a shadow play with his hands. Going further, he might use glove-puppets and then marionettes. Extending his resources still further, he might rope in others to assist, telling them what movements and sounds to make. From there it is a short step to the conventions of theater and cinema. Through the successive extensions the teller tells his tale – he simply uses more and more elaborate means to tell it.[63]

Two concepts Currie uses in the above outline of his view need explicating straightaway before we can deal with it adequately: these are the concepts of "make-believe" and the "fictional author." First let me say a word about the former.

Following Kendall Walton, in his influential book, *Mimesis as Make-Believe*,[64] Currie understands the author of a fictional work as intending its reader to "take a certain attitude toward the propositions uttered in the course of his performance," which Walton likes to compare with the attitude of children in games of pretend or make-believe. It is, Currie says, "the attitude we often describe as, rather vaguely, in terms of 'imaginative involvement' or (better) 'make-believe.' We are intended by the author to *make-believe* that the story as uttered is true."[65] Currie gives full acknowledgement to the influence of Walton on his position with regard to make-believe, but warns that he departs from Walton on various points, including the notion that "we can *define* fiction itself in terms of the author's intention concerning our make-believe," which Walton denies.[66]

I myself am not very much inclined towards the theory of make-believe. But my own inclination in this regard, and the theory of make-believe itself, can be put aside for present purposes. Whether or not a make-believe theory of fiction is correct will have no implications for the view of silent reading being developed here.

As for the concept of the fictional author, it is Currie's view that our experience of fictional story-telling is best understood as the experience not of the author's telling us his story but of some character's doing so, of whom it is fictionally true that he or she is the author of the story being told. This fictional author is not to be confused with the fictional narrator of the story, who may or may not be identified. As well, according to some literary theorists, novels like *Emma*, where there is no named or otherwise identified narrator, are assumed to have an "implied" narrator, whose fictional persona can be gleaned from the manner in which the story is told.

Again my inclination differs from Currie's. For I am much inclined to think that it is the real author whom I experience as the teller of the tale, which he or she may also tell, by means of a designated or implied narrator. However, a lot of what I am trying to say in this study is, I think, consistent with the concept of a fictional author. So those who are devoted to that concept should not, on that account, put my book down as hopelessly misguided.

What, then, does Currie have right? Why am I bringing him into my argument?

What I think Currie has right is something very obvious: perhaps so obvious that we tend to forget it, and need the kind of reminder Currie gives. But obvious though it may be, it is also very important. It is, simply, that narrative fiction is *story-telling*, whatever form it takes: whether it is a tale told round the campfire, which we must not forget the *Iliad* must originally have been, a performance of Ion the rhapsode, a servant reading to his master or his master reading aloud to himself before the age of silent reading, the Elizabethan at the Globe theater, the movie-goer at the Thalia, or any one of us curled up with a good (or bad) book. It's all story telling, however else you might want to look at it. "Through the successive extensions the teller tells his tale – he simply uses more and more elaborate means to tell it."

All this is not to say, I hasten to add, that I agree with Currie's analysis of what exactly goes on in our experience of the movies: what, to put it another way, the "phenomenology" of our movie experience is, as opposed to that of our reading experience. But this is not the place to go into it. What suffices for present purposes is to re-emphasize Currie's observation that movies, plays, novels, and other forms of literary fiction are instances of story-telling, and story-tellings must have storytellers.

Behind every story, then, there is a storyteller, whether you think of that individual as the author of the fiction, a fictional author, or, to mention another possibility, suggested by William Irwin, an "author construct," which is to say, "a theorist's conception of the author, particularly as this conception applies to interpretation."[67] As I said before, my own inclination is to construe the "ultimate" storyteller as the author, and find myself in complete agreement with a recent statement of what I take to be the quite commonsensical view that "unless there is some particular reason for thinking otherwise, I see no problem with the intuitive view that the person telling the story is the one who made it up . . .."[68] But however we construe that personage in the reading experience, we do all agree that the imaginary presence of a storyteller is essential to that experience. *Someone* is telling the story. Well, what of *that*?

Let us return, again, to Ion the rhapsode. Ion tells stories. More exactly, he tells the Homeric stories of the *Iliad* and *Odyssey* – in Homer's language, of course. (For the time being I will leave out the added complication that he also, in the process of telling the stories, makes "critical" comments on them; but I will return to this very important aspect of Ion's performance later on.)

But, really, it is somewhat misleading to say that Ion "tells stories," because it suggests that Ion is making them up himself. Rather, he is "reciting" stories that were already made up, and written down. For simplicity's sake, let's say that there really was a single poet, Homer, who wrote the *Iliad* and *Odyssey*. And let's say that Homer is telling us these stories through his texts via Ion. If you are a proponent of the fictional author, or the author construct, you may substitute either one for Homer, or any other author who may come up in what follows.

What exactly then is Ion doing? It appears to me that the best way to describe it is that Ion is "playing the role" of Homer: he is impersonating the storyteller – not of course in the sense of an imposter, passing himself off as someone else for purposes of deception, but in the sense of an actor or actress impersonating a character in a play, playing a part. Ion, after all, is a performer; and his performance, I am suggesting, consists in representing, as an actor, the teller of the *Iliad* and *Odyssey* stories, whether you conceive of that storyteller as Homer, or the fictional author, or the author construct.

But Plato makes it very plain in Book III of the *Republic*, as we have already seen, that the storyteller's style is not a simple affair; and from this it follows that the rhapsode, as impersonator of the storyteller, must, in his style of performance, reflect the complex style of the storyteller, if he is to be successful. The complexity is this: "narration may be either simple narration, or imitation, or a union of the two."[69] In simple narration, the storyteller just tells what happened in his own voice: as Plato puts it, "the poet is speaking in his own person; he never leads us to suppose that he is anyone else." Whereas in mimetic narration, the poet "says" the words of the characters themselves. Again, to quote Plato, "when the poet speaks in the person of another, may we not say that he assimilates his style to that of the person who, as he informs you, is going to speak?" [70] And in the combination of the two, simple and mimetic narration, the poet sometimes narrates in a straightforward manner, in his own voice, sometimes mimetically, in the voices of his characters. As Plato portrays the occurrences of these three styles in the literary works of his own times, "poetry and mythology are, in some cases, wholly imitative – instances of this are supplied by tragedy and comedy; there is likewise the opposite style, in which the poet is the only speaker – of this dithyramb affords the best example; and the combination of both is found in epic, and in several other styles of poetry."[71]

The wholly imitative style of narrative does not concern us here. It is the style, of course, of dramatic representation, tragic and comic plays, as Plato says, which, I suppose, is not in the rhapsode's line of work. So in regard to performances, we need only concern ourselves with simple narration, or with the mixed mode, narration cum imitation: that is, narration in which the storyteller, in his own person, tells what happened, and, from time to time, impersonates the characters by reciting the words that, according to the story, they spoke. But it must be emphasized that even when Ion is impersonating the characters whose speeches he speaks, he is also still representing the teller of the story; for the teller of the story, be he author, fictional author, or author construct, is telling the story both by telling what happened and by quoting what the characters said. So when Ion recites the *Iliad*, he gives an impersonation of the teller of the tale; and *part* of his impersonation of the teller of the tale consists in his impersonating the characters by reciting their speeches. Or, perhaps more accurately, when he recites the characters' speeches, he is impersonating the storyteller impersonating the characters by reciting their speeches, much as in *Hamlet*, in the play within the play, the actor who plays "the actor" impersonates an actor impersonating a king: an impersonator of an impersonator.

Now of course all I can do is imagine what Ion's performance must have been like, with the little help, always bearing in mind a negative, censorious tone, that Plato gives. But I have, after all, heard reciters of stories myself. For example, and much to the present point, I once heard a tape of a great actress – Julie Harris, I think it was – reading *Jane Eyre* aloud. Needless to say, she read the simple narration with great expression; and when she came to reciting the speeches of the dramatis personae, she declaimed them as an actor or actress would have if performing in a play. That is how I think of Ion's performance, minus, of course, the sound imitations, and, more important, his critical comments on the text he was reciting. In any case, I think we all know what kind of a performance reading a story aloud to others is like, whether it is a mother reading *Winnie the Pooh* to her child, someone reading ghost stories around the campfire, or, if you are fortunate enough, hearing Julie Harris reading *Jane Eyre*.

To continue in this vein for a moment more, if my *a priori* history is anywhere near the truth, reading fiction to yourself was, for a long time, reading it aloud to yourself. In doing so you, like Ion or Julie Harris, were playing a part: you were impersonating the teller of the story: the author, or fictional author, or author construct. When one read fiction aloud to oneself prior to the era of silent reading, did one read "with expression"? Who can say? We are not to the manner born. But if you try doing it, I think you will find, as I said previously, that unless you make a special effort to read in an expressionless monotone, like a court recorder reading back testimony, you will, quite naturally, read *con espressione*. I think that unless you are autistic, or making a special effort, you will, perhaps unconsciously, make a performance of it. Of course you will not achieve the results of a Julie Harris, or an Ion. But you will, I suggest, be doing, and producing something of the same kind.

At this point it seems more than time that the specific thesis of this monograph should finally be stated. The eighteenth century was right, *pace* Burke et al. *Silent reading is a performance.* They were wrong of course about what *kind* of performance it is. But that it *is* a kind of performance they had exactly right.

What kind of performance silent reading is will occupy us in what follows. And it cannot come as much of a surprise to the reader that once the eighteenth-century answer, the Addisonian answer, is rejected, the most obvious candidate for the position must be musical performance, and the silent reading of the musical score.

This possibility, and its problems, are what I wish to explore.

I am not, to be sure, the first to draw the analogy between reading and performance, or between novel-reading and score-reading; at this writing I am aware of six persons who have pursued, or at least entertained the idea, none of them extensively. All deserve discussion before I get on with my analysis.

13 Predecessors

In an enticing aside, Edward T. Cone wrote, in *The Composer's Voice*, "as in music, reading is a kind of performance, albeit a silent one."[72] But an enticing aside it remained, never to be developed further by him, although he was ideally qualified, as a musical performer and musical commentator, to develop his thought.

Nelson Goodman briefly considers the possibility of construing silent readings of literary works as instances of them, but pretty much dismisses the idea out of hand. Brief as it is, however, his discussion (not surprisingly) is worth our attention.

Goodman begins with the assertion that "what the writer produces is ultimate; the text is not merely a means to oral readings as a score is a means to performances in music."[73] With regard to the modern institution of silent reading, this is of course partly true, although not true with regard to the long tradition, which I have discussed above, of read-aloud literature, in the considerable period of time before silent reading prevailed. But the reason I say it is only partly true is that, if what I have been arguing in these pages is right, what the writer of silently read fiction produces, namely, the text, is *not*, as Goodman puts it, "ultimate." What is ultimate is the performance of reading; and in that respect it is, like the musical score, "a means to performance . . .."

"We might," Goodman continues, " try to make literature into a two-stage art by considering the silent readings to be the end-products, or the instances of a work; but then the lookings at a picture and the listenings to a performance would qualify equally as end-products, or instances, so that painting as well as literature would be two-stage and music three-stage."[74] This is obviously intended to be a *reductio* of the notion that a silent novel-reading, for instance, could be considered an "instance" or "end-product" of the work. It fails to be, I think, because Goodman fails to be sufficiently clear about what a silent "reading" amounts to and what relation it bears to a musical "listening."

Consider, first, what Goodman calls a "listening" to a musical performance. Clearly, there are two things here: the listening and the performance. We all agree to this distinction; but it does not lead us to conclude that music is a three-stage art. It is two-stage: work and performance thereof.

But what about the "reading" of a novel? What makes this a less obvious case of the same thing is that it is less obvious that here, as well as in the case of musical listening, there are also two things: the performance of silent reading and the experience of that performance. The difficulty of course is that they are the same event under two different descriptions, because, unlike in the case of musical performance, the performer and the audience are one and the same individual, and the "reading" both the reading as performance and the reading as the experience thereof. And what helps us to accept this is, first, the analogy with a pianist (say) playing a sonata to herself, where she is performer and audience in one, and, second, the silent reader of a musical score who, just like the silent reader of a novel, is both the silent performer of the work and, at the same time, the silent auditor of it.

Thus, if we keep clear the distinction between silent "reading" as experience of the work, and silent "reading" as performance of the work, there will cease to be the apparent disanalogy between music and silently read literature that is supposed to generate Goodman's *reductio*, which is, I think, the point Barbara Herrnstein Smith was making when she wrote that "Although, in a silent reading, the performer and audience are necessarily the same person, this should not obscure the fact that the reading consists of two theoretically distinct activities, only one of which is comparable to listening to music or looking at a picture . . .. [I]f we can conceive of the solitary singer enjoying his own performance, we should not really have any trouble extending the conception to the solitary silent reader."[75]

I have not, however, gone on here to consider Goodman's suggestion that painting must become a two-stage art of works and "lookings," if literature becomes one of works and "readings." In other words, I have not considered the possibility of the autographic visual arts as performing arts. But I will take that question up later on.

But to return to Professor Smith, her correct diagnosis of the silent reading experience as a kind of performance is, it seems to me, marred by an unnecessarily obscure account of, if I may so put it, the performance "product." She writes: "The reader is required to produce, from his correct 'spelling' of a spatial array of marks upon a page, a temporally organized and otherwise defined structure of sounds – or, if you like, pseudo-sounds."[76]

Richard Shusterman, in a critique of Smith's view, is quite right in being perplexed, as I am, by the notion of "pseudo-sound." "Is it perhaps a voiceless mouthing or merely a mental mouthing, or perhaps just a cerebral flutter?"[77] His suggestions are, I take it, supposed to be a *reductio* of her view. And they surely are if we take the view that the performing product is pseudo-sound.

But silent reading no more results in something called "pseudo-sound" than reading a musical score does; nor does reading a description of Anna Karenina result in a "pseudo-sight." A score reader hears sounds in his head, musical sounds; he neither hears nor produces pseudo-sounds, whatever they might be. And if one hears, say, a fictional character speaking in one's head, one hears speaking sounds, not pseudo-sounds. Pseudo-sounds are a red herring, and need trouble us no longer.

But another objection of Shusterman's, to Smith's notion of reading as performance, and, by implication, to mine as well, needs to be addressed. Shusterman writes:

> However, the most important objection to Mrs. Smith's defence of literature as a performing art is that it violates and perverts the established notion of performance in the performing arts. In all the traditional performing arts, performance is a public affair, a spatiotemporal event which can serve as the common object of criticism . . . . But the performance of pseudo-sounds in one's head or nervous system when one reads silently to oneself is hardly the same kind of performance for it is private and inaccessible . . . .. [We] may very justly object that since the notion of performance is essentially different in the traditional performing arts, Mrs. Smith's notion of silent literary performance does not warrant the assimilation of literature to these performing arts, and thus to speak of literature as essentially a performing art is misleading.[78]

Shusterman's objection, in its most general form, is simply that reading to oneself is different from the things we call "performances" in the *recognized* performing arts.

But stated so generally, it has little merit. The whole point of the exercise is to argue that we should come to see reading to oneself as a performance, even though we had not seen it that way before. It is to argue that the differences are superficial, and that there is a deep affinity between silent reading and performing, which, if we recognize it, will illuminate the activity of silent reading as an artistic practice.

This kind of argument is hardly unfamiliar to philosophers, and is, indeed, one of the staples of the profession. There is nothing wrong with it, *per se*, as a strategic move. It may, of course, be bad philosophy in the individual case, if the identity suggested is infelicitous. But that must be determined on independent grounds; and it is yet to be determined, with regard to the identity in question, namely, silently read fiction as a performing art.

To be fair to Shusterman, though, his argument is not couched in such general form. There is a more specific claim about the differences between silent reading and performance, properly so-called, which amounts to saying that there is an *essential* difference between silent reading and performance. And if, indeed, there is an essential difference, then, obviously, the two cannot be equated. The claim is this: that "In all the traditional performing arts, performance is a public affair, a spatiotemporal event which can serve as a common object of criticism," whereas the performance in one's head "when one reads silently to oneself is hardly the same kind of performance for it is private and inaccessible."

Now I will be discussing some aspects of criticism, as they apply to silent reading of fiction, later on in this study. But it would be well to answer Shusterman's specific argument in this place. Let us work our way, to that end, through three kinds of "performing to oneself," the third being, on my view, silently reading to oneself works of fiction.

It is quite clear that playing to oneself on the piano, a sonata of Beethoven's, is granted on all hands to be a *bona fide* case of performance, even though the performer and the audience are one and the same person. And it is abundantly clear that such a performance, although neither intended nor offered as a "public object," is potentially hearable, "in principle observable," and hence a possible object of criticism.

The crucial step is from playing a sonata to yourself to silently reading a sonata score to yourself. If this latter is accepted as a silent performance in the head, then the way is at least partially cleared to the acceptance of silent fiction-reading as a silent performance in the head as well. And, surely, there is a powerful *prima facie* case for score-reading as an internal performance. It is the way it has always been described by those few who can do it, which is why the definition quoted previously reads as it does: "The internal realization of the sound of a work by means of simply reading the score."

But is the *prima facie* case adequate? Will not silent score-reading as internal performance be vulnerable to Shusterman's objection that being a private object, it is not open to criticism, as we expect performances to be? I do not think so. For although the silent performance of a sonata in the head, by score-reading, is not hearable, it is *potentially* hearable in that another token of its type, that is, the *performance*'s type, could be produced in the normal way, and criticized in the normal way.

Once the second step is accepted, the third, to silent reading as performance, if not inevitable (which I do not claim), is at least initially plausible. But if silent score-reading as performance is not vulnerable to Shusterman's objection that, being a private object, it is not open to criticism, surely, it will be apparent, silent fiction-reading as performance will be. For whereas the normal way to experience music is in public performance, not in silent reading, the normal way of experiencing the novel (say) is in silent reading, not in public performance. So what could it possibly mean to say, as I did with regard to silent score-reading, that the silent performance in the head, of a novel, although not hearable, is potentially hearable in that another token of its type, that is the *performance*'s type, could be produced in the normal way? For the normal way of experiencing a novel, unlike a musical work, is *not* in public performance.

To begin with, *of course* the normal way of experiencing a novel is not in a public performance, as it would be for a play, or an epic poem in ancient Greece. If it were, there would be no need for a philosopher of art to have to *argue* that it is, *au fond*, a performing art after all, even though it is not usually experienced in public performances. For *obviously*, plays and ancient epic poetry *are* performing arts. That the novel and other forms of silently read fiction are *different* in that respect goes without saying.

Furthermore, it is, of course, possible for even a normal reader to read a novel, or a passage thereof, aloud to someone else. And so one can claim, I suppose, that any silent reading of a novel is potentially a public performance, if another token of its type is read aloud, and, therefore potentially an object of criticism. But more plausibly, one makes public one's "performances" of novels by talking to others about how they understand them, and their understandings, surely, are open to criticism. (More of that anon.)

But I rather think that the important question to be asked about silent fiction-reading as performance is not whether criticism, point for point, can be applied to it as to the recognized performing arts. Rather, the question to be asked is whether *enough* of what we think of as criticism will survive if silent fiction-reading is thought of, the way I am now urging, as a form of performance. My answer is yes, and it will be argued for in the pages to come.

Interestingly enough, another of Shusterman's objections to the notion of silent reading as performance, which he apparently thinks is not of the first importance, is, to my mind, the most demanding of our critical notice. It is that if reading fiction were a silent performance of sounds in the head, then "people born deaf could not read or at least not appreciate literature, since they cannot recognize or imagine the sounds that would be heard if the work were read aloud . . .."[79] This point too I must put off until the appropriate place in this study, where it will be dealt with in the detail it deserves.

Now there may be something of the *Zeitgeist* playing itself out in the emergence of interest in the ontology of art in Goodman's *Languages of Art*. For in the very same year of its appearance, another soon to become "classic" in the field was published: Richard Wollheim's *Art and Its Objects*. And Wollheim, in this book, comes very close to considering the possibility of "readings" as "performances," although he never decisively takes the step. What he has to say, however, is well worth considering for a moment.

The ontological status of what Goodman had denominated the "allographic" arts is a question that emerges very close to the beginning of *Art and Its Objects* (although Wollheim could not at that time have been aware of Goodman's terminology). And the direction Wollheim's argument is going to take is very clear right from the get-go. "That there is a physical object that can be identified as *Ulysses* or *Der Rosenkavalier*," Wollheim avers, "is not a view that can long survive the demand that we should pick out or point to that object."[80]

The physical object hypothesis being rejected summarily, Wollheim's proposal, with regard to the allographic arts, was that they are to be understood in terms of the type/token relation. In what follows I am going to consider this proposal only as it applies to music and the literary arts, the only ones relevant here. But it should not go without saying that these are not the only arts for which the type/token relation was thought by Wollheim to be at least a possible model.

In Sections 35–39 of *Art and Its Objects*, Wollheim explores the logical niceties of classes, types, and universals, before settling on types as the most likely candidates for musical and literary works. The logical niceties are not my particular concern right now so I will simply cut to the chase. Wollheim poses the question, "What are the characteristic circumstances in which we postulate a type?," adding the caveat that "The question, we must appreciate, is entirely conceptual: it is a question about the structure of our language." And he answers the question as follows: "A very important set of circumstances in which we postulate types – perhaps a central set, in the sense that it may be possible to explain the remaining circumstances by reference to them – is where we can correlate a class of particulars with a piece of human invention: these particulars may then be regarded as tokens of a certain type."[81] And from here, as Wollheim sees it, it is an easy and obvious step to the conclusion that the type/token relation is the proper one for the allographic arts. "It will be clear," he concludes, "that the preceding characterization of a type and its tokens offers us a framework within which we can (at any rate roughly) understand the logical status of things like operas, ballets, poems, etchings, etc. . . ."[82]

Having come this far with Wollheim, it is the most natural thing in the world to conclude that in the performing arts the work is the type, the performances of it its tokens. But what of literature? Here Wollheim seems to have been of two minds. To see this, we must return to Section 6 of *Art and Its Objects*, from which I quoted earlier, in which Wollheim was introducing his reader to the idea that some works of art clearly cannot be identified with a physical object. He wrote, in emphasizing this point, that: "There is, of course, the copy of *Ulysses* that is on my table before me now, there is the performance of *Der Rosenkavalier* that I will go to tonight, and both these two things may (with some latitude, it is true, in the case of the performance) be regarded as physical objects. Furthermore, a common way of referring to these objects is by saying things like '*Ulysses* is on my table,' 'I shall see *Rosenkavalier* tonight': from which it would be tempting (but erroneous) to conclude that *Ulysses* just is my copy of it, *Rosenkavalier* just is tonight's performance."[83]

Of course the obvious point of the passage is that there are lots of copies of *Ulysses* besides Wollheim's, lots of performances of *Rosenkavalier* besides tonight's performance. Something, however, about the example is jarring, and what it is is immediately perceived if we put on Wollheim's table, alongside *Ulysses*, a score of *Rosenkavalier* and an edition of *Hamlet*. For now Wollheim's copy of *Ulysses* sticks out like the proverbial sore thumb. There are, indeed, many copies of *Ulysses* besides his, many copies of the *Rosenkavalier* score besides his, many copies of *Hamlet* besides his. As well, there are many performances of *Rosenkavalier* besides the one he will go to tonight, many performances of *Hamlet* besides the performance he went to last night. But now the analogy breaks down, because there are not many performances of *Ulysses*: since the novel is not a performing art, there are no performances at all: and thus literature seems to have two ontological faces.

Wollheim obviously noticed this anomaly and took it into acount when he introduced later on the type/token distinction for the allographic arts. For he wrote: "it might be argued that, if the tokens of a certain poem are the many different inscriptions that occur in books reproducing the word order of the poem's manuscript, then, 'strictly speaking,' the tokens of an opera must be the various pieces of sheet music or printed scores that reproduce the composer's holograph. Alternatively, if we insist that it is the performances of the opera that are the tokens, then, it is argued, it must be the many readings or 'voicings' of the poem that are *its* tokens."[84]

Now it may seem like an absolutely trivial point, but I hope to convince you otherwise in a moment, that the problematic literary art in Section 6 was the *novel*, for which *Ulysses* was the stand-in, whereas here, in Section 36, it is the *poem*. And Wollheim is quite consistent in this. For in the second edition of *Art and Its Objects*, he alludes to this question again in one of the supplementary essays, where he writes that "for several arts (poetry, music) whose works are indubitably types it is debatable what are the tokens of these types."[85]

It is apparent, then, that Wollheim was at least considering the possibility that *readings* might be the tokens of literary works, although various copies of their texts remained another possibility for him. But what kind of tokens *are* "readings"? Well, if the symmetry between read literature, and music, and drama, is to be maintained, it is going to have to turn out that readings are at least a limiting case of *performances*. I am willing to take that step; that is what this book is all about. But was Wollheim willing to take it?

It is with the above question that the significance of the change from novels to poems in Wollheim's text begins to make sense, at least to me. For poems, after all, lead a kind of double life for us. We read them to ourselves, and we go to poetry readings as well. And in the good old days we used to read them aloud in the family circle. So the art of poetry, as it exists today, is a kind of half-way house between-out-and out performed literature and private, silently read literature, of which the modern novel is the prime exemplar. It seems natural, therefore, that when Wollheim came at least to consider the possibility of read literature as a performing art, as he *appears* to have done in Section 36 of *Art and Its Objects*, he should, perhaps unconsciously, have substituted the poem for the novel as his literary example. It is easier to conceive of the poem than the novel as a performing art.

That Wollheim *was* considering not only the possibility of something other than text copies being the tokens of poetic work-types, but that he was considering the possibility that *some* of them at least might be *performances* is strongly suggested by his putting it that the tokens of a poetic work-type might be the poem's "many readings or 'voicings,'" with *voicings* in scare quotes. It certainly sounds as if by "voicings" Wollheim meant readings of poems aloud, in the form of recitations, although in a moment I will suggest another alternative, not perhaps for what Wollheim meant but for what I would mean.

In any event, Wollheim did not pursue further the possibility of silently read fiction as a performance art, as I am doing now, although he did acknowledge it *as* a possibility. But, as a matter of fact, the *way* Wollheim presented the possibility, in Section 36 of *Art and Its Objects*, is highly suggestive of how one might work one's passage from readings as tokens of literary work-types to *performing-tokens* of them. So let me return to it again, briefly, for another look.

Wollheim entertained the possibility of poem-tokens being the poem's "many readings or 'voicings,'" and put *voicings* in scare quotes. My question now is *why* Wollheim should have put it this way: in particular, why "voicings" and why in scare quotes? Surely the more obvious, not to say more idiomatic way of putting it would have been "their many readings and recitations." One reads or recites a poem – or, of course, listens to recitations of them.

Let us remind ourselves that the history of silent reading is a long and complicated story. But even when reading poetry silently to yourself became widespread, poetry remained and remains a literary form in which the sound of language is an integral part, as it is not, in the case of the novel, to anywhere near the degree to which it is in poetic texts. What this means is that even when you read a poem silently to yourself, you must, in your reading, "hear" the sound of the poem in your mind's ear, be very conscious, in other words, of its sound if it were recited. The way *I* might express the thought is to say that a poem must, even when not recited, be "voiced," in scare quotes – "voiced" in the mind's ear. I will not go so far as to say that that is what Wollheim meant when *he* wrote that the tokens of poems might be their "voicings," in scare quotes. I do not think it was. But it is what *I* would mean; and I am grateful to Wollheim for the hint.

But I said earlier that poetry might serve as a kind of half-way house between out-front performed literature and private, silently read literature, of which the modern novel is the prime exemplar. I think we can now see why.

If, when we read poetry silently to ourselves, we "voice" in our heads, as described above, we are, in effect, having a performance in our heads: our performance to ourselves. And this, if true, is not an isolated case of silent sonic performance in the head. It is simply the verbal analogue of the phenomenon of score-reading, already discussed, in which the musician, silently perusing her score, hears a performance in her head of the musical composition that is scored.

But if hearing poetry in the head, when reading it silently, seems plausible to you, because of the intimate connection between the poetic text and the sounds of the linguistic utterances it inscribes, and because of the analogy of silent poetry reading, in this respect, to the silent reading of the musical score, then perhaps I can encourage you to take the next step with me, since the consideration of poetry puts you half way there. It is the step that takes you to the conclusion that silently read prose fiction is a performance art as well: that the readings of novels are not only tokens of work-types but *performance*-tokens of them: that they are, in fact, like silent poetry readings, "voicings" in the head. That, of course, is the thesis of this monograph, to be developed in what follows.

Finally, an interesting, but nevertheless little developed exploration of the possible relation between score-reading and novel-reading is to be found in J. O. Urmson's elegant little essay titled, simply, "Literature."[86]

Urmson accepts, as I have done, the difference in ontological status between arts that require the performer as intermediary, like music and drama, and the arts, like painting and sculpture, that, so to speak, we confront directly, face to face. And he too finds silently read literature, such as the novel, apparently, "at least at first sight, to be anomalous with respect to this classification." For "there seem to be no executant artists or performers here: who could such artists be?" And yet "we cannot readily assimilate literature to sculpture and painting."[87] Silently read literature seems to have fallen between two ontological stools.

At this point Urmson proposes the hypothesis, which I wish to pursue, "that, contrary to first appearances, literature is in principle a performing art," and, more specifically, "that, in reading a literary work to oneself, one is simultaneously performer and audience, just as when one plays a piece of music to oneself."[88] And he points out, as well, as I have done, that, after all, Western literature comes out of an oral tradition.

> If we consider such a work as the *Iliad*, there is good reason to believe that before writing was known to the Greeks there were bards who had learned the poem by heart and who went around giving performances of it, or of excerpts from it . . . .. It is not implausible to think of the *Iliad* as having been written down, probably in the seventh century BC, as a set of instructions, as a score for bards. It is fairly certain that Herodotus wrote his *Histories* as a score and that people first got to know them by hearing public performances.[89]

As is already apparent, from the passage just quoted, Urmson conceives of a score as a "set of instructions" for a musical performance, and the written text of the *Iliad*, in its first incarnation, as a "score." It therefore comes as no great surprise that he then draws the analogy between reading music and reading words. "Now I suggest that learning to read an ordinary language is like learning to read a score silently to oneself."[90] In other words, when we learn to read (silently), we achieve the same *result* as when we read a score (silently): a hearing "in the head."

What would seem the next obvious step would be to construe silent reading as a silent performance, to oneself, just as silent reading of a score to oneself might be construed as a silent performance to oneself. *But Urmson does not take the step*; in this, it seems to me, he misses the full potential of the insight he has so elegantly laid out in his brief essay. Why he falters here needs to be considered.

Urmson, quite rightly, recognizes that there are various reasons for reading a score (silently) at various levels of score-reading proficiency. But I do not think he characterizes correctly what "optimal" score-reading is like: what exactly it results in. This can be seen, in part, from the way he slides from the description of scores as "instructions" for performance to them as "recipes," with the analogy to cookery recipes in mind. Musical score-reading, at the optimal level, Urmson says, "is the reading of a recipe or set of instructions with the ability to recognize what would result from following them." And he adds, right away: "I am reliably informed that experienced cooks may acquire the same skill; they may be able to read the recipe and recognize what the confection would taste like."[91]

It is the analogy between musician as score reader and cook as recipe reader that is the villain. And to see this we had better see how Urmson cashes it out. He writes:

> It would be implausible to say that musical score readers are giving a per-formance to themselves or that readers of cookery recipes are preparing a private and immaterial feast. Apart from the fact that they need hear no sound (they may or may not hum to themselves), considered, absurdly, as performances, what they do would be intolerably bad. They habitually read through the slower bits far faster than they perfectly well know the music should go, and, for many reasons, nobody can read a fast complex piece at a speed that he recognizes to be that of the music.[92]

Now one is certainly obliged to agree with Urmson that reading a cookery recipe cannot produce tastes in the head, even to the most experienced and gifted practitioner of the art. But that is precisely where the analogy between musical scores and recipes in cookery books breaks down. And if one wishes to describe scores as recipes for performance, as Urmson does, one had better be fairly clear that there are recipes and "recipes." There are, one must suppose, profound differences between the sense modali-ties of taste and hearing, and (therefore) profound differences between the symbol system that is the musical score and the symbol system that is the recipe for chicken soup.

Indeed, the kind of musical notation that best fits the description of instructions or recipe for performance is not the musical score, but the tablature, which just is a set of instructions for where to place your fingers, on a fretted instrument, for example, to achieve a performance of the piece it notates, whereas a score is a spatial representation of a musical work: of a complex sonic event. It is only the latter, not the former, that can be read to achieve a mental performance. The tablature, like the recipe for a dish, is not meant to be read, nor can it be, for pleasure, but only for practice: or, to be more exact, the recipe reading does not constitute a pleasurable *culinary* experience, nor the reading of the tablature a pleasurable *musical* one, whatever *other* pleasure the reading of either might bring

Of course one must concede that there are practical limits to how complex a musical composition can be for its score to still be susceptible of a silent reading that produces a completely satisfactory performance in the head. But that being said, it must be insisted, *pace* Urmson, that there is nothing "implausible" in describing the results of score-reading, by the likes of a Beethoven or a Brahms, as anything less than "a performance to themselves." Composers and conductors have described them as such, nor is there any evidence for Urmson's claim that slow movements are necessarily read faster than what is the correct tempo, or fast movements slower, again, within reasonable limits, when the purpose of the reading is not careful study of the work but a "musical experience" of it. And even if it were, at times, necessary to read a movement at a slower tempo than intended, that might make it a bad performance, but hardly a non-performance. Few can achieve the experience of a musical performance through score-reading alone; but those that can *do.*

There is, I suppose, a good deal of truth in Urmson's description of the accomplished recipe reader not as eating a dish in her head but merely recognizing or being able to anticipate what it would taste like: "If I add this and this and this, the texture will be something between a pudding and a mousse." And that is *sometimes* all that the musician gets or wants to get from her reading of a score: "If I do this and this and this, I will get just the right balance between the winds and the strings." (She is preparing to conduct the work.) But it is a mistake to think that, like the recipe reader, that is all she *can* get. What *she*, the musician, can get, if she has the musical mind and training for it, is a full performance in the head. (I will be going into that more deeply in a moment.)

And if that is so – if the optimal score reader can get a full performance in the head – then, if we are to press to its ultimate conclusion the analogy between silent reading of musical scores and silent reading of novels, we will have to be prepared to accept the notion that what silent reading of the novel produces in the head is a performance in the fullest sense of the word. Urmson was not prepared to take that final step. His description falls short of calling the result of silent novel-reading a "performance." Rather, he says: "We read to find out how the performance will go and are then content."[93] But if the result of reading a novel is a full-blooded "performance" in the head, we have a need to ask, as I suggested earlier, what *kind* of a performance it really *is*. We know what a musical performance is in the head because we know what it is out of the head. Novels, however, were never meant to have performances out of the head, so we do not have, in the novel, external performances of them to help us characterize the inner performance, as we have in the case of score-reading. That silent readings of novels are performances in the head must be argued for; and what kind of performances they are must be explained. All of this is yet to come.

14 The Ion Within

The Addisonians came a cropper because they tried to make out that silent reading produces a kind of theatrical performance before "the mind's eye." But there are two convincing reasons to reject this theory, as we have seen. First, simple introspection reveals that a running display of mental "images" is palpably not what the silent reader of novels and other fictional narratives experiences. And, second, the theory, anyway, has a faulty foundation, which is the Lockean model of language. The Lockean model has it that descriptive utterances and texts evoke in hearer or reader perception-like experiences of the visual kind. In general, however, this model cannot be accurate; so the Addisonian theory of read literature cannot be accurate either, for it is motivated by that very linguistic model. Not to worry, though: a far more reasonable theory of silently read literature as a performing art is available to us. It is, put baldly, that we ourselves are performers, and silent reading our performing art. We are all, when we read novels, silent Ions. *We* impersonate the storyteller silently, as Ion does out loud.

This notion requires, of course, some spelling out. And the first clarification I want to make is to distance myself from the theory of make-believe. When I say that the silent reader "impersonates" the storyteller, I do not mean to say that she makes believe she is the storyteller. I mean, as in the case of Ion, or Julie Harris, that she "plays the part" of the storyteller, as the actor "plays the part" of Hamlet. I do not think that playing the part of Hamlet is the same thing as making believe one is Hamlet. Likewise,

I do not think that when the silent reader is playing the part of the story-teller, she is making believe she is the storyteller.

That having been said, I want now to return briefly to the two genres of novel I discussed early on: the letter novel, and the novel that presents itself in the form of a diary, journal, or something else of that kind. They both now require a brief re-examination, in light of what has transpired since.

I said, it will be recalled, that when one reads a letter novel, *Pamela*, for example, one enacts or impersonates a letter-reader; and when one reads a diary or journal novel, one enacts or impersonates a diary- or journal-reader. We now see that that is not *strictly* true. What I impersonate or enact is the storyteller telling his story through the representation of letters or diary. I enact or impersonate the storyteller reading aloud the letters or diary. That, it appears to me, is the most accurate way of putting the matter. And if, in the letters or diary, the fictional writer of same quotes some other character of the fiction, then I am enacting or impersonating the storyteller enacting, within his recitation of the letters or diary, the speeches quoted therein.

But I said earlier that we have a right to imagine Ion the rhapsode as an expressive player of the storyteller role he has taken on. His "straight" narration is expressively spoken; and he speaks the characters' speeches in a dramatic manner, as an actor on the stage. What, then, are we to say of the silent reader's performance (for performance is exactly what I am saying the act of silently reading a novel is)? Does it make any sense at all to assert that a silent reader reads *expressively*? Can one silent reader read more *expressively* than another? Does *that* make sense? And if it doesn't, does it make any sense to refer to silent readers as silent declaimers? Certainly there are better and worse readers aloud. Julie Harris was certainly better at it than my mother. Are there better and worse silent readers? I think the answers to all of these questions are affirmative, though this surely needs argument. We can begin that argument by returning once again to the silent reading of musical scores.

15 The Eloquence of Silence

The silent reading of musical scores, at the level of competence that can result in a performance, in the head, is a rare accomplishment that, one must assume, can rest only with musicians at the very pinnacle of the profession. And when you are a good enough musician to do that, a Mozart or a Beethoven, or a major league performer, I think we are justified in assuming that what you hear in the head will be a "musical" performance: that is to say, a musically expressive, eloquent one.

Of course the style of the performance such a master will hear in the head will vary with the score-reader. Doubtless, Mendelssohn would have heard a Romantic performance of Mozart's Jupiter Symphony if he were to read the score of that work; and it is reasonable to believe Beethoven would have heard Handel's works, when he read the scores, as we are told he did, on his deathbed, in the style of performance suited to his own genius and period, not the style in which they were performed by Handel and his contemporaries. The point is that when someone is a good enough musician to read a score and, thereby, perform the music in the head, he will also be a good enough musician to have a firm conception of how the music is to be performed: how it goes. He will hear in his head a performance with a style; a performance with a particular expression; very likely, if the score-reader is a Mendelssohn or Beethoven, an eloquent performance.

Silent readers of scores, at the level I am talking about, which is the level necessary for doing the thing at all, are all performers on at least one musical instrument. Being experienced performers, they will all have definite, and perhaps divergent ideas of how the music of Mozart or Bach or Mahler is supposed to be performed. And so their in-the-head performances will, no doubt, bear the stamp of their sonic performance. That being the case, a word is in order about musical performance in general before we go on.

The way I view musical performance, a musical performer is, as the common phrase has it, a "performing *artist*." She is an artist whose artwork is the performance she produces on her instrument.[94]

A performance is a *version* of the work performed. And in order for a performer to produce a credible performance, a credible version or "reading" of the work, she must have an *interpretation* of it. She must have her own idea of how the music goes: what makes it tick. She bases her performance on that idea; on that interpretation. Her performance, then, literally displays forth her interpretation. If she had a facility with words she could tell us what her interpretation of the work is, as an analyst or theorist might. But in any event, one can show an interpretation as well as tell it, as we have seen. And what the musical performer does is to show her interpretation through her performance. That is why a particular performer's rendition of a work is sometimes called by music reviewers her interpretation of it: so-and-so's "reading" of the *Hammerklavier* Sonata or the Italian Concerto.

As well, it is necessary to point out, before I go on, that one of the most admired skills of the musical performer, among fellow musicians, is what is known in the trade as "sight-reading," the skill (and art) of reading musical notes, and realizing them on the spot in a correct performance of a piece you have never played or heard before. Prodigious feats of reading at sight, among the immortals, are the stock in trade of musical biographies. But unlike the skill of reading scores and hearing, thereby, performances in the head, sight-reading is an accomplishment that even the amateur performer can achieve at a fairly acceptable level.

Now it might seem, to pursue the matter of playing at sight a bit further, that the best a good sight reader can hope to achieve is playing the notes correctly, most of the time. A "musical" performance, an expressive, sensitive, eloquent performance – that could scarcely be possible. For, as I made clear before, a reasonably successful performance requires that the performer have an interpretation of the piece on which such a performance can be based: a take on how the music goes, what makes it tick. But, it would seem, it could hardly be possible to have an interpretation of a work one has never played or heard or seen before. So a reading at sight, it seems to follow, can only be an adequate rendering of the notes, never an expressive, sensitive, "musical" performance.

Nothing, however, could be farther from the truth. For sight-reading itself, as an activity, would not even be possible if the sight-reader were not intimately acquainted with the musical styles of the composers whose works she plays at sight, or familiar at least with their contemporaries. So if a pianist has put before her a sonata by Haydn she has never seen, played, or heard before, she does not know how that particular sonata goes, what makes it tick; she does not yet really have an interpretation of *it*. But she certainly knows classical style in general; and that knowledge not only makes it possible for her to read at sight, without mistakes, the sonata in front of her; it also makes it possible for her to play it well: to play it musically, expressively, with eloquence. A good sight-reader is someone who can play even very difficult works at sight and get most of the notes right. A *really good* sight-reader is someone who can also do it musically, expressively, with eloquence.

Now, to return to score-reading – to reading a score and hearing a performance in the head – the same distinction will be in place, between reading at sight and performing a piece you already know and have rehearsed. Brahms was once, so the story goes, invited out to a performance of *Don Giovanni*. He is supposed to have replied, pointing to the score, "Why should I go out when I can hear a better performance at home?" We have good reason to suppose that he was well acquainted with Mozart's masterpiece; and so when he read his score he was hearing in his head a "rehearsed" performance. He was not reading at sight. But when Beethoven was occupied, on his deathbed, with reading the scores of Handel that an English admirer had sent him as a gift, he was, most of the time, reading scores with which he was not familiar, since most of Handel's works, during Beethoven's lifetime, were unperformed and forgotten. Beethoven was reading Handel's works, and performing them at sight, in his head. Nevertheless, I am sure they were magnificently "performed." I wish I could have "tuned in."

It is my thesis that in silent reading of fictional works, I am a performer, my reading a performance of the work. It is a silent performance, in the head. I am enacting, silently, the part of the storyteller. I am a silent Ion. The most direct analogy, I claim, is between the silent reading of a novel and the silent reading of a musical score. It is an analogy I rejected earlier because we did not have to hand, then, the correct notion of what the performance is. Now we do. It is not a movie or a play in the mind's eye: it is a story telling in the mind's ear. There is an Ion in each of us whom we enact in silent reading of fictional narration. We hear stories in the head, the way Beethoven, when he read the scores of Handel, heard musical performances in the head.

How far can the analogy be taken? I think it works pretty well.

I begin by pointing out that the choice of Beethoven reading the scores of Handel over Brahms reading the score of *Don Giovanni* was quite self-conscious and premeditated. Beethoven was reading at first sight; and that, more often than not, is what the silent reader of fictional works is doing. It seems to me, at least, that we tend to listen over again to the same pieces of music far more than we tend to read over again the same novels and stories. (Narrative poetry is a different matter, and I will leave it out of the picture, although the repeated reading of fictional works, of whatever kind, poses no particular problem for the thesis being developed here.) That being the case, the analogy to be drawn is between the first reading of a score (that one has never heard) and the first reading of a novel.

But who is the reader we are considering? As we have seen, the score reader, if he is at the level of competence that enables him to hear a performance of a symphony in the head, is a quite extraordinary individual. He must possess musical training: it is neither the skill nor training of amateurs, or even professionals of the "lower orders."

Such is not the case, needless to say, with regard to the novel reader. Novel readers vary in degree of sophistication from the child reading his first storybook to Harold Bloom or Lionel Trilling reading *Finnegans Wake*. But in contrast to the truly competent reader of musical scores, the truly competent reader of novels need hardly be either gifted in the literary arts or professionally trained to read and understand literary texts, although, presumably, one of the tasks of college literature departments is (or should be) to impart to the liberal arts student additional knowledge and skills, beyond mere literacy, for the future enhancement of his or her literary appreciation. Thus, in this respect, there certainly is a *disanalogy* between reading scores and reading novels. It is not, however, a disanalogy damaging to my project, and I will say no more about it.

But the question is still outstanding: Who is the novel reader about whom I will be talking? Here is a sketch. I want my novel reader to be someone with at least a significant degree of literary sensibility. By that I mean someone who not only reads a detective novel or a spy thriller to pass the time on a train or plane with a diverting story, but someone who can actually be moved by literary characters, by literary language, and by the other "beauties" of more distinguished literary works.

Furthermore, my novel reader will be someone in whose life the reading of novels occupies a significant place. I do not mean that he be an obsessive reader: someone who scorns all forms of "trivial" amusement, refuses to own a television set, and spends every moment of his spare time devouring books. But he *is* someone who spends some significant portion of his time reading fiction, and feels the need to return to the activity if the press of business and other of life's vexations have kept him from it for any considerable length of time.

As well, my novel reader is someone who enjoys a wide range of genres and forms. He does not scorn the shilling-shocker, the lower kinds of sci fi, spy thrillers, and other kinds of time-wasters. But he also feels the need, at times, to read the "good stuff": Dickens, and Jane Austen, and serious contemporary works. In addition, he reads novels that are supposed to "make one think": that is to say, fictional narrations that not only tell a story but have as one of their literary purposes presenting (and perhaps *defending*) a philosophical, moral, political, or other important thesis, about which the reader is supposed to think, and which may even have a lasting effect on him. (I shall return to this point later on.)

And, finally, the novel reader about whom I will be speaking is someone who is serious enough about the enterprise to spend at least a little of his time reading literary criticism. He need hardly be a literary scholar with a PhD in English. Large critical tomes need not be his steady diet. Book reviews and articles in the popular press will do for him. But I do need a reader with enough interest and sophistication to not only read good novels but to read *about* them sometimes as well. And that is because if I can't find a role for literary criticism in my account of reading as performance, I think we would have to conclude that the account is defective.

So if I am to work literary criticism into the equation I must be able to talk about a reader who reads it (unless I can find some distant, and less plausible connection between reading and criticism, which I am loath to attempt).

With this sketch of my competent novel reader in mind we are now ready to pursue further the analogy between reading scores and reading novels, and, more generally, the analogy between reading and recitation. And here are some questions we have outstanding.

A read score is a performance in the head. But score-reading is the province of superbly trained and supremely gifted musicians. Because of that, their performances (in the head) are going to have style, expression, eloquence, and all of those things that make performances notable, different from one another, and better or worse than one another. Read novels, on the other hand, are performances in the head not by professional actors or declaimers, not by professors of English literature or professional critics. Rather, they are performances in the head, mental story telling by ordinary readers. So what worries us is whether it makes sense to say that *their* performances have style, expression, eloquence; whether it makes sense to say that one such reader's reading is better or worse than another's. For if it doesn't make sense, then it would seem doubtful that the analogy between novel-reading and score-reading, musical performance in the head and silent reading as performance in the head, will really stand up.

I think that all of these matters revolve around the role of interpretation in performance. So we will have to take another look at that. But before we do, we might, at this point in the discussion, want to return briefly to silent play and script reading, which was a pivotal case, to see if we want to revise somewhat our outlook on that in light of what progress we have so far made with the question of silent novel-reading.

16 Radio Plays

It will be recalled that dramatic texts were compared with musical scores, and the conclusion drawn that even though their ontologies seemed to match – script is to play performance as score is to musical performance – their silent readings were markedly different. First, silent playreading is something any literate person can do, whereas silent score-reading is reserved for the gifted few, even among the musically literate. Second, and most important, a musical score enables one to fully realize a musical performance in the head, whereas a printed play does not. In particular, the visual aspects of a dramatic performance are under-determined by the printed text, and, in any case, our visual imagination cannot do the comparable job that our aural imagination can, in the case of the musical score. Language simply does not hook up with visual imagery the way musical notation does with the aural imagination. The criterion of success in score-reading is a complete performance in the head, so I claimed, but the criterion of success in play-reading is merely "comprehension."

However, I am now suggesting that the silent reading of a novel consists in hearing a performance in the head of a recitation: a story telling. And if I can hear the narrative voice in the head, in reading a novel silently to myself, why can I not hear in my head the dramatic voices of a silently read play? Would this not begin to make play-reading more like score-reading than I heretofore wanted to allow?

One might want to compare the silent reading of a play with a black-and-white movie. A black-and-white movie is still a visual representation of a story – but minus, of course, the colors. A silent reading of *Hamlet* is a performance of the play heard, but not seen, in the head. It is a performance of the play nonetheless, albeit minus an important part – the visual aspect, just as the black-and-white movie is a "play production," though lacking the colors.

Those old enough will doubtless be reminded, by these ruminations, of the "radio play." For radio provided a format for dramatic performances that made them, of course, performances only in sound. There were, in the radio days, performances, much abridged because of time constraints, of various of the literary masterpieces. And there were also plays written expressly for the radio medium, that sought to make artistic use of its "limitations," the masters of this short-lived artistic genre being the unjustly forgotten Arch Oboler, and the well-remembered Orson Welles. Why not say, then, that the silent reading of a dramatic text produces a "radio play" in the head? This would put the experience of silent play-reading somewhere between that of silent score-reading and silent novel-reading.

I am not averse to such a suggestion, as it does not materially affect my conclusions about silent novel-reading, which is my principal topic. But it might be well to amend it somewhat by pointing out that there might be *two* ways of experiencing a silently read play, one pushing it in the direction of silent score-reading, the other in the direction of silent novel-reading.

Let us suppose that I had the ability to actually hear in my aural imagination particular performers playing the roles of the characters in the play I was reading: Richard Burton as Hamlet, Hume Cronyn as Polonius, and so on. In that case my reading would be something like the silent reading of a score, where the reader heard the separate instruments of a symphony orchestra as those of a particular group of players.

On the other hand, the reader of the play might be thought, rather, to be hearing in her head a reader of the play, herself, reading the play to her. In that case she would be hearing a narrative voice that was, as Plato would put it, telling a story in the purely imitative, mimetic style (which he so disapproved of): never saying in her own voice what is happening, but telling the story entirely in quotation marks. In that case, the silent play-reading would be exactly like the silent reading of a novel: a recitation in the head. Except, of course, that the novel-reciting inner voice is likely to be giving a "mixed" narrative, which is to say, part straight narrative, part quotational, or a purely narrative performance, without quotation.

There is, I am sure, far more to be said than I have done, about the silent reading of plays. But as it is tangential to my main purpose, I will leave things now as they are. Silent play-reading is something of a back-water for me; and I now want to re-enter the main stream of my argument, which, as I have said, leads us again to the topic of interpretation.

17 Silent Interpretation

There are a great many books and articles on the topic of literary interpre-tation, not to mention interpretation in general, and in other specialized areas, and I have nothing to add to that debate. Rather, I am going to take a certain vague, I think uncontroversial, concept of interpretation for granted, and hope that my reader shares it with me. What this concept is will be both implicit and, at times, explicit in what I say.

I said earlier, when I was talking about musical performance, that a musical performance both is an interpretation, and is based upon an inter-pretation. It is the showing of the interpretation it is based upon.

Now we had no problem in thinking of score readers as hearing in the head interpretation-driven performances. Score readers are highly trained, gifted, and experienced musicians, musical performers in their own right, at the professional level, who know the nuts and bolts of the compositions they perform and of the scores that they read and realize in silent per-formance. Likewise, Ion, Julie Harris, and their ilk are talented, seasoned performers. They have the talent and the know-how to "get into" their roles as reciters. All of these folks can be assumed to have interpretations of the works they perform, either out loud or in silence.

But ordinary readers of novels, even the above-average ones I am dealing with, are not "professional" novel readers (whatever that would mean).

They are not writers, book reviewers, literary critics, or professors of English literature. They are people with various occupations, in various stations of life, who have in common the love of literature, and time to satisfy their appetite for it. Does it make sense to say of these folks that they have *interpretations* of the novels they read, and that their readings of novels are interpretation-driven performances in something like the way score readers have interpretations of the musical works they read, which drive their performances in the head? I think it does make a good deal of sense, although it is not altogether obvious, and requires spelling out.

I think it is obvious – common sense, if you like – that when I read a novel (and I will mean, from now on, unless otherwise stipulated, reading a novel for the first time) I am interpreting it as I go along. I take it that I cannot really understand what is going on in a novel, in any deep or nontrivial way, without an interpretation of what is going on as well.

Now there is a good deal of debate not only about what interpretation is, but about what is susceptible of interpretation in the first place. Directly relevant to what I am now discussing, it is sometimes claimed that you can't interpret the "obvious": that is to say, interpretation starts with a difficulty. What one cannot immediately understand must be interpreted. "Well, that, after all, is a matter of interpretation," signifies something that presents a problem to the understanding, and about the meaning of which "Reasonable persons might disagree." Paul Thom puts the point insightfully in his book, *Making Sense*, where he writes: "In order for the process of interpretation to get going someone has to judge that the object is somehow deficient and someone has to desire that this lack be supplemented."[95]

Thus, although understanding a novel isn't all interpretation, one cannot, at any significant level, understand a novel without interpretation. One understands many sentences in a novel without interpreting them: the obvious presents no difficulty, and difficulty is what interpretation is required to overcome. As Thom puts it, the object of interpretation is judged insufficient, and interpretation is called in to fill the void.

Now various objects present various insufficiencies to interpretation. The insufficiency that novels present for interpretation is insufficiency of *meaning*. This kind of insufficiency is illustrated by Thom's example of "the handwriting on the wall": "when Belshazzar classified the marks on the wall as *writing*, he thought of them as having the type of significance possessed by a communication (having been written by a hand). But as soon as it was so classified, the writing posed a puzzle insofar as its significance could not be grasped. Further interpretation was therefore necessary."[96] The marks on the wall were insufficient as to meaning, which is to say, simply, Belshazzar could not understand them, under the assumption that they were writing. Daniel, the interpreter, repaired that insufficiency by supplying their meaning, through interpretation.

Daniel as interpreter introduces a useful (and pretty obvious) distinction that will serve us well in what follows. The reader of the novel, in the process of reading, is an interpreter of the novel. But he may, at times, call in a Daniel to his aid. In that case he may be adopting someone else's interpretation. I will begin by considering the reader of the novel as his own interpreter. I will then go on to talk about the role in his reading of the "outside" interpreter, which is to say, the literary critic.

The reader of a novel must, of course, understand what she is reading. Part of that understanding will be the function of mere linguistic competence: understanding the obvious. But part of that understanding will be interpretation: making good the insufficiency of meaning.

Some of the reader's interpretational skill will be exercised upon the meaning of sentences that may present difficulties. But a more considerable part will be exercised rather upon the larger meanings of the work as a whole as well as the larger meanings and aesthetic or artistic functions of its parts. The nuts and bolts of interpretation are, needless to say, highly controversial. They are, however, not my subject: they are the affair of the "philosopher of interpretation," of which there are many. What I must do is to try to show how, given a very general understanding of what interpretation is, we can work it into the thesis that reading is a form of performance in the manner of the score reader's interpretation-driven musical performance in the head.

To begin with, we must remind ourselves that novel readers are usually "sight readers": that is to say, they are generally reading a novel in hand for the first time. So they do not have interpretations of the novels they are reading at-the-ready, prior to the performance of reading, unless, of course, they have taken the trouble of reading interpretations of the works first. Let us assume that they have not.

But just like musical readers at sight, readers of novels are not without preconceived ideas of how what they are about to read will go. If I have read *Great Expectations* and *David Copperfield*, I will not be clueless when I pick up *Bleak House* for the first time.

Nevertheless, unlike the musical sight reader and reader of scores, the novel reader has no professional training in the interpretation of the art works she is "reading at sight." Should this trouble us? I do not think so.

For the reader of whom I am speaking, the interpretation of literature is a practice: an example of what Gilbert Ryle famously called "knowing how," as opposed to "knowing that."[97] As a practice, it is learned *in* practice. And that practice starts early on.

The first "serious" literary work I can remember reading was *Les Misérables*. I was late in learning how to read, and I think I must have been about twelve years old when my mother, who was a voracious reader herself, and refused to read "trash," hurled a copy of Hugo's masterpiece at me while I was lying in bed, out from school with "the grippe" and spending this luxurious, "stolen" time listening to the soaps on my radio. "Improve your mind, for God's sake," she said, or words to that effect, as the mind-improving missile landed at my feet.

Well, even a twelve-year-old can, eventually, become bored with Stella Dallas and Mary Noble, Back-Stage Wife; so I imagine it was out of sheer boredom that I did, reluctantly, pick up *Les Misérables*, only to become totally enthralled by the story, much to my surprise. But not only was I enthralled: I think I was deeply moved, to the extent, anyway, that a somewhat spoiled kid of my age in my circumstances could be. Furthermore, I think I not only understood the narrative; as well, I think I at least had a vague idea that the narrative "had something important to say;" that it wasn't just an enthralling story but a story that was "making a point." In short, I think I was being introduced, without, of course, being aware of what was happening, to a "moral dilemma."

I had been brought up to believe that it was wrong to break the law: I had certainly learned from The Shadow, as had my contemporaries, that "The weed of crime bears bitter fruit. Crime does not pay." I was also raised in a "socially conscious" family and school environment, and knew that it was wrong for people to be hungry and in want. So I was well prepared to contemplate the moral dilemma presented to me by the narrative, even though I may not have been prepared to describe it as such, and didn't know a Kantian from a consequentialist. In short, I had been equipped with the concepts necessary for *interpreting* at least part of the story of *Les Misérables* in social and moral terms, if at a childish level, prior to my picking up the book. Had I not been, I can't imagine I *could* have been enthralled by the narrative.

Now I am sure all readers of novels, of the level of sophistication I am assuming, had similar experiences to mine as children. So I am confident that they will accept what seems to me to be the incontrovertible premise that we gradually develop, through education, experience, and parental guidance, interpretational skills enabling us to read with understanding. No doubt my readers, or at least many of them, are not yet convinced that silent novel-reading is a kind of performance. But I think I have at least made out my case that a necessary condition for novel-reading's being *interpretation*-driven performance, namely, the ability to interpret as one reads, is developed naturally, in the proper environment, through practice, not precept, without the need of formal instruction to that end. And having given the example I have of my experience with *Les Misérables*, I think I can rely on my reader to add his or her own, and imagine the many other examples that might be adduced, without my having to go any farther in that direction.

But there is more to say about my own example, before I go on. What I am urging about my first reading of Hugo's novel, at the age of twelve, is that it was, even at that tender age, an interpretation-driven, silent performance: a story telling in the head. Suppose, though, I had not first read the work when a child, but, rather, read it for the first time as an adult. Wouldn't it be fair to say that my reading as an adult would be a "better" reading? It would be a reading with more understanding, more perceptivity, a more highly developed emotional and moral sensibility, wider and deeper knowledge of the literary tradition into which it fits, and so forth. Furthermore, since I understand silent novel-reading to be a performance of story telling in the head, I feel quite confident in describing the adult reading as a "better performance" than the reading of a twelve-year-old.

The reason this conclusion is important, of course, is that the notion of one reading of a novel being better than another, in the sense of one performance of a musical work being better than another, or Julie Harris' recitation of *Jane Eyre* being better than the ordinary person's, seems problematic. And if it were, then the analogy between silent novel-reading and performance would break down. But now we see that it makes perfect sense to think of a silent-reading-as-performance being better, *qua* performance, than another silent-reading-as-performance. It makes perfect sense to think of one's performances of silent reading improving over time. It makes perfect sense to think that there are some people with finer literary sensibilities than others, and, hence, able to achieve better reading "performances" than others. I certainly enjoy my "performances" of the novels I read. I should not, on that account, think that there aren't others who, because of inborn talent, more experience, or greater knowledge, produce better, or more enjoyable silent performances of novels, for themselves, than I can produce for myself. All of this, if correctly put, starts sounding like common sense, rather than a philosopher's fantasy, although, needless to say, what makes one reading performance better than another, and the relation between "better" and "more enjoyable," raise deep philosophical questions.

Talk of better and worse novel-readings, and of improving one's own over time, raises the question of how improvement occurs. One way, of course, as I have already suggested, is simply by experience: by continued reading of fictional works. Another obvious way is by reading what others,

the literary critics, have to say about literary works. I have nothing profound or new to say about this, merely the obvious. But the obvious needs
to be said to make sure the omission does not come back to haunt me later
on. So here it is.

18 The Critic's Role

I once wrote, with regard to literary criticism: "The job of the critic,
like the job of the [musical] performer is to make the work available for
appreciation."[98] What I had in mind at this stage of my thinking about
the reading experience was a disanalogy, rather than an analogy, between
reading and performance. Here is how that argument went.[99]

The ability to read musical scores, unlike the ability to read novels and
other forms of literary fiction, as I have emphasized on previous pages, is
not widespread, but a very rare commodity. The music-lover, therefore,
unlike the lover of fiction, requires an intermediary, which is to say, the
musical performer: "by far the vast majority of us require the performer
to, so to speak, be the middle man between us and the work."[100]

But the novel reader is not, like the musical listener, unable to make the
work available to herself. The ability to read novels at an adequate level of
comprehension is widespread, and attainable through practice, in ordinary
life, under ordinary circumstances. Nevertheless, there *are* those who have
made a profession out of acquiring deeper understanding of fictional literature than even the sophisticated reader-for-pleasure has achieved. These
are the literary critics. And the sophisticated reader-for-pleasure may, at
times, seek out critical writings to broaden and deepen her understanding and reading experiences of the work in hand. When she does this, the
critic is making available to her whole works, or aspects of works, which
have not been available to her heretofore. In so doing, my argument went,
the literary critic is serving the function, *vis-à-vis* the reader-for-pleasure,
that the musical performer is serving, *vis-à-vis* the musical listener. And if
the critic is an interpreter, then it is no wonder that the performer is called
an "interpreter" as well. For the critic is a performer in both cases.

Now it is not that I want to repudiate this analogy. As far as it goes,
it works. But it tends to lead us away from the more important analogy
between reading and musical performance that it has been the purpose of
this monograph to draw: the analogy between silent reading of a score,
which produces a silent musical performance in the head, and the silent
reading of a novel, which produces a silent literary performance in the
head, namely, a silent recitation of a story: a silent story-telling. In *this*

analogy, the function of the critic is the same for both terms: the critic, in each case, is serving a performer. What service does he provide?

Traditionally, the critic's job has been divided into an evaluative and an interpretive part, although it has always been agreed that in practice they cannot be cleanly prised apart. I will concentrate here on the critic's job as interpreter.

When the performer goes to the interpreter, it is, presumably, for help in forming or improving his performance. A performance, remember, is interpretation-driven. I must understand how it goes and, where appropriate, what it means, to give a credible and creditable rendition. When I have a problem in either department, I may seek the interpreter's help. When I accept a part or the whole of the critic's interpretation, I make it *my* interpretation, as I do when I accept my own interpretation as adequate or good. As Thom puts it, "For me to adopt an interpretation is for me to make it mine."[101]

As I said earlier, I am considering on these pages only first readings of novels. In first readings, unlike prepared and rehearsed musical performances, a critic's interpretation of the work in question, even if it is read prior to the first reading of the novel, cannot serve the function of *being* the reader's, that is, performer's interpretation, prior to the performance of the reading. For it cannot at that stage have been made the reader's own, since the reader does not yet know how the critic's interpretation will match up with his, that is, the reader's experience of the work. It can, of course, influence, help to direct the reading of the work, and can, in the process of reading the work, be made, in whole or part, the reader's own. But the reader cannot have an interpretation of the work, prior to his first reading, the way a pianist, who has studied and rehearsed a sonata, can have an interpretation of the work, prior to walking out on stage to play it, that drives her performance. The reader's performance is interpretation-driven *as he goes along*, as the interpretation develops in lock step with his reading. It cannot be a preconceived performance plan that the reader is following, as it can for the prepared musical performance.

However, a novel reader's acquaintance with the critical literature, either literature about an author, or genre, or whatever, prior to her reading a given work, can certainly have a powerful influence on what interpretation will develop as she reads, and, as well, in retrospect, on what interpretation she may develop *after* she reads. (I shall have a good deal more to say about what happens *after* one reads a little later on.)

At this point, then, we have a very general idea, which is all the idea we really need, for present purposes, of how literary criticism functions in the experience of silent reading, when silent reading is understood, as I am arguing it should be, as a performance in the head. The general point is that there is no special problem with understanding what contribution literary criticism makes to the silent performance of literature, any more than there is a special problem with understanding what contribution music theory and analysis make to the silent performance of music.[102] All offer up to the silent performer interpretations that she can accept, accept in part, reject, or use to help in forming her own interpretations. And with this general account in hand, I want now to turn to another matter, of potential difficulty for the position being developed here.

19 Readings as Art

Perhaps the most glaring *disanalogy* between readings of novels and performances of musical works is revealed by what we might call the *second* way of describing musical performances. Performers are called *interpreters* of what they perform; and that, as we have seen, causes us no trouble. Readers of novels, whether sophisticated or naive are rightly, appropriately thought of as interpreters of what they read.

But if we are to take the description "performing artist" seriously, when it is applied, as it normally is, to at least the great and admired virtuoso performers of our musical tradition, then we seem compelled to see their performances as "works of art" in their own right, apart from the art works they are performances of. And if, furthermore, we are to take seriously the analogy between musical performance (in the head, via score-reading) and the silent reading of literary fiction, as I am doing on these pages, then we seem to be driven to the conclusion that readings of novels are art works in *their* own right, apart from the art works they are readings of, since we are committed to the thought that musical performances in the head are works of art. The argument seems altogether straightforward. Performances are art works; readings of novels are performances; therefore readings of novels are art works. Straightforward, yes; however, one seems forced to admit, clearly absurd. My reading of *Pride and Prejudice* an art work? Surely we have here a *reductio ad absurdum* of the claim that silent readings of literary fiction are performances.

One possible option here is simply to deny that performers are artists, from which it directly follows that their products, performances, are not works of art. The problem instantly dissolves. And if it be responded that this option runs roughshod over common art-world discourse, in which performers *are* frequently referred to as artists, "performing artists," there is a counter-response readily available. We do, after all, call various practitioners of skills or crafts "artists," in what R. G. Collingwood called the "courtesy" sense of the word.[103] When a pastry chef or taxi driver performs his task particularly well, and, perhaps, with a bit of style or panache, we call him an "artist" in the kitchen or at the wheel. But we surely don't mean that he is *literally* an *artist*, or his product *art*. We are, rather, paying him and his work an extravagant compliment. Similarly, so the argument goes, when we call performers "performing artists," as indeed we are wont to do, we do not mean it *literally*. We are simply saying: "You are really very very good at what you do."

Perhaps there are some who would find this response attractive. I do not, and I devoted a good deal of time in my book on musical performance, *Authenticities*, to insisting that performers are indeed, literally, performing *artists*, their products, literally, works of *art*.[104] I do not believe this conclusion can reasonably be avoided: the notion of performers as performing "artists" in the literal sense of the word is too deeply imbedded in our aesthetic discourse to be dislodged in so facile a manner. So I must try to show how this fact is compatible with the thesis that novel-readings are performances. And before I do that I must, briefly, give the reader some idea of what *kind* of artist I take a performing artist to be, as well as what kind of an art work I take it to be that he or she produces.

As we saw earlier, performers of musical works are interpreters of them, as readers of novels must, as well, be interpreters of what they read. In order to perform a musical work properly, one must have an interpretation of it: which is to say, an idea of "how it goes," "what makes it tick." And, of course, if you are the performer of a work with semantic content, if you are an actor, say, or an opera singer, you must have an interpretation of what the meaning is of the work you are performing. But we will stick here with absolute music, which will bring out more directly the points I am about to make.

A good or distinguished performer on a musical instrument, then, is an interpreter of what she plays; and this in two senses. She *has* an interpretation of what she plays, how it goes, what makes it tick, even if she can't verbalize it; *and* she *shows, displays* her interpretation in her performances. She is not a teller of interpretations; she is a *shower* of them.

Of course performers vary in their interpretations of the works they play, in both senses of interpretation: their notions of how the work goes, what makes it tick, may vary, and so, too, by consequence, will the showings of their interpretations, i.e. their performances. And we mark this fact in our discourse by referring to them as this or that performer's "version" of this or that work: Horowitz's or Serkin's or Emanuel Ax's "version" of the *Pathétique*, for example.

Seen in this way, as "versions" of works, performances find an analogy in another musical category, the "arrangement." Johannes Brahms, as is well known, composed his famous Variations on a Theme by Haydn in two "versions," the first for two pianos, the second a "version" arranged for orchestra. They bear the same opus number, 52, to indicate that they are the same work, not two different ones; but they bear the designations 52a and 52b to indicate that they are, indeed, *different* versions of the *same* work: one work, two versions. And in orchestrating his piano variations, Brahms was exercising and exhibiting "artistry": the artistry of the musical "arranger."

On a less exalted plane, the musical world is full of musical works, arranged by people who specialize in this sort of thing, for instruments other than the ones intended by their composers: arrangements of string and piano works for winds, arrangements of concertos for instruments other than the ones originally intended, and so on. And in all of these instances the people who do this are, to a greater or lesser extent, exercising and exhibiting the artistry of the musical arranger. Their arrangements, like performances, are works of art in their own right, apart from the works of which they are the arrangements. Like performers, as well, arrangers are interpreters in both senses of the word. In order to make successful arrangements they must have interpretations of the works they arrange; they must have an understanding, an interpretation, of how the works go, what makes them tick. And their arrangements display forth these interpretations.

It appears, then, that one way to view performers is as "arrangers" of the musical works they perform. Like arrangers, they present "versions" of works, *their* versions, based on their interpretations. Performers are the kind of artists arrangers are. Both produce art works – but, of course, art works parasitic on the pre-existent art works they perform or arrange.

The problem, then, for present concerns, is this. If silent readings of fictional works are analogized to musical performances, then they should be seen as art works in the sense just outlined above. They are "versions" of the works they are readings of, which is to say, performances of; and, by consequence, art works in their own right, apart from the literary works they are readings, performances of. And surely that seems highly counter-intuitive, if not absurd. Why?

Below I list some of the beliefs or, if you like, "gut feelings" I suspect are driving the intuition that silent readings of literary fiction cannot be art works (or performances).

(a) Silent readings of fictional works are internal, private events, whereas art works are public objects of perception; so silent readings of fictional works, therefore, cannot be art works. (We have seen this objection before.)

(b) Silent readings of fictional works are ordinary, everyday sorts of things, whereas art works are very special, outstanding sorts of things; so silent readings of fictional works just aren't important enough, out-standing enough things, if you will, to count, therefore, as art works.

(c) Readers of fictional works are ordinary, everyday sorts of people, whereas artists are very special, outstanding sorts of people; so silent readers of fictional works just aren't important enough, outstanding enough people, if you will, to count, therefore, as artists.

I do not think that (a) should give us much trouble, if indeed it is driving our intuition that silent readings of literary fiction cannot be art works properly so called. For although art works usually, normally are public objects, there are more than enough obvious exceptions to defeat the claim that a necessary condition for being an art work is being open to public scrutiny. As is well known, Mozart, for example, was capable of compos-ing large-scale musical works "in his head," that resided there, complete, until such time as he "copied" them out into musical notation. And there seems no reason to claim they weren't works of art until scored. But if you require a less extravagant example, merely consider Collingwood's claim that when a poet composes a simple verse in his head, or a composer a simple melody, these are already fully fledged little art works, whether or not they ever become public objects.[105]

Of course all of these examples are of art works in the head that *can* become public objects. But even if that makes a difference, so too, after all, can my silent reading of a novel, if I wish to read aloud. So all in all there is nothing in (a) that should, when considered aright, feed anyone's intuition that silent readings cannot be art works. That being the case, let us move on.

Conjectures (b) and (c) are, of course, intimately related. For, obviously, if silent readings of literary fiction are not art works, then silent readers of literary fiction are not artists (*qua* silent readers); and if silent readers of lit-erary fiction are not artists, on the grounds given, then silent readings of literary fiction are not art works (*qua* silent readings).

Now whether or not silent readings of literary fiction are art works, given the skeptical doubts expressed in (b), opens a huge can of worms. For the most obvious way of answering it is to first say what makes some-thing a work of art, which is to say, supply a "definition" of "art," and then determine whether silent readings of literary fiction fall under that definition or not. But the definition of art is the most disputed question in contemporary philosophy of art, and has been since the beginning of the twentieth century. Clearly, attempting to provide a definition of "art" here would take us on a journey far distant from my present concerns, and one that, in any case, I am not at this time in a position to complete. A more modest strategy, then, must be found.

Another possible strategy, considerably less ambitious, would be to canvass some of the more prominent theories of what art is that have been propounded in the past fifty or one hundred years, formalist theory, expression theory, aesthetic attitude theory, institutional theory, and so on, and, in each individual case, determine whether or not silent readings of literary fiction do or do not fall under the definition that particular theory provides. That procedure, although clearly inconclusive, since there is no guarantee that any of those theories is correct, or that an exhaustive survey has been made, would at least give us some substantial evidence as to whether or not silent readings of literary fiction were in the aesthetic ball park. But like the previously suggested strategy, it would be too time-consuming and, as well, lead us too far afield.

A third strategy, and the one I shall adopt, is far more modest and tractable, although far from conclusive. What I propose doing here is simply to look at some examples of the more peripheral things that we are more or less agreed upon are performances, and at least minimal performance art works, or border-line art works, and try to determine whether silent readings of literary fiction are any less probable candidates for art status than these. I shall suggest that they are not. From, this I shall further suggest, it follows directly that it is also no less probable to think of silent readers as performing artists.

But as a preliminary to that, I want to bring into the picture yet again what I suppose to be a kind of evolution of the silent reading of literary fiction from the oral performance and audition of public, read-aloud literary fiction. I will suggest it is reasonable to suppose, without committing the genetic fallacy, that some of the performance aspects of the latter have "rubbed off," or exist, at least in a vestigal form, in the former.

It must be noted, straightaway, that we should not confuse the question of whether something is of greater, or lesser, or minimal value with the question of whether it is *art*. For if we have learned anything in the past fifty years about definitions of art, it is that they are definitions of *art*, not of good art or great art or valuable art, and must allow as art, works that run the entire gamut from the worthless to the exalted. So our question is not about the worth of silent readings; rather, it is about the plausibility of construing them as performance art works, whatever their value as such might or might not be.

That being said, let us return for a moment to our earlier theme of the transition from fictional literature as an overtly performing art, in the long period before the advent of silent reading, to the present state of play. What I want to emphasize here, or, perhaps, re-emphasize, if it has not come through loud and clear, is how *long* a period it really was during which the art of fictional literature was a performing art in overt, unequivocal form, and how recent the culture of silently read fiction really is. I put such emphasis on this fact to try to break down the traditional distinction between performed literary arts, such as drama, and silently read literary arts, of which the novel is, of course, the prime exemplar. As I have put the point previously, silently read fictional literature and performed literature are not two parallel streams from antiquity, but one stream, the performing one, that diverged into two in the recent modern era.

Let me propose what I hope is not too far fetched an analogy. Imagine the conceptual shift that takes place when you stop seeing the whale as a fish and start seeing it as a mammal. Seen as a fish, it is seen in stark contrast to tigers, rats, chimpanzees, and elephants. But once one sees it as descended from some species of the class Mammalia, and itself a species of that class, for all its differences from its land-dwelling relatives, one begins, of course, to see similarities rather than differences: for example, appendages cease to be seen as "fins" and are seen instead as vestigial "limbs."

Given, then, that the silent reading of literary fiction has evolved from a performance oriented literary fiction, might we not expect to find lingering in the descended species vestigial, as well as full-blown characteristics of its ancestor? And might we not expect, in particular, that various silent readings of fictional literature would run the gamut from what we might want to call vestigial performance art works to those that we might want to acknowledge as full-blown ones, remembering that this is not a value ascription but a descriptive one.

Furthermore, we can, as I suggested above, try to make this more plausible by looking at some other borderline cases of performance that might raise similar questions with regard to their status as performance art works, or lack thereof – questions that have nothing to do with the "peculiar" case of silent fiction-readings.

Consider some examples:

(i)   A seal playing "My Country 'Tis of Thee" on a set of horns (an old circus stunt).

(ii) A nine-year-old, talentless child playing the usual pieces from the *Anna Magdalena Bach Notebook* at his first music-school recital.

(iii)   A very musical, clearly quite talented nine-year-old child playing the same pieces under the same circumstances.

(iv)   My whistling themes from *Carmen* on the way to class.

And just so we don't stick exclusively to music:

(v)   A nine-year-old child with little talent playing Tiny Tim in the class Christmas play.

(vi)   Mickey Rooney playing Puck in the Hollywood version of *A Midsummer Night's Dream*.

(vii)   A nine-year-old child reciting a poem by Robert Frost from memory as a class assignment.

(viii)   Julie Harris reading aloud *Jane Eyre* at a recording session.

Are these performances? Are they performance works of art? All? Some? None?

Example (i) is uncontroversial. *Of course* the seal's "performance" is not a *performance*, even though "My Country 'Tis of Thee" is quite recognizable (if rhythmically disjointed). A performance at the very least is the action and product of a conscious, intentional agent, which the seal obviously is not. And not being a performance it is not, by consequence, a performance art work.

Example (ii), however, is already problematic, and obviously far removed from the seal's "performance," however unsatisfactory it may be, artistically speaking. But is it a performance, and is it art?

The talentless juvenile pianist, like the seal, has, doubtless, learned pretty much by rote to play "the right notes"; and he probably has little, if any understanding of the pieces he is playing. Whatever in the way of an "interpretation" he may have, if that is not too strong a word for it, has been imparted to him by his teacher, with no understanding of it on his part. But, after all, he is not a seal. He knows what he is doing, even though he is far from fully *understanding* what he is doing.

I think it is a toss-up whether we want to call what he has produced a performance or not, and if not, certainly not a work of performance art either; and the same would, no doubt, be true of examples (v) and (vii) as well: the nine-year-old Tiny Tim and the nine-year-old's recitation of Robert Frost. We might, if we wanted to be generous, call these proto-performances; or, and I have no quarrel with this, not performances at all. And as performance art works the same alternative decisions seem appropriate.

But examples (iii) and (vi) are quite another matter. Here we have *talented* juveniles; and however much such performances may rely on their mentors for guidance of a more or less strict kind, the performers are doing something that their untalented counterparts cannot do. But what is it that they *can* do? Well, all of those undefinable things that make us want to call their products true performance art works. The talented young pianist does not "just play the notes" but plays "with feeling." As well, she does understand, at her level, *what* she is playing: she has an interpretation, if perhaps a derivative one, and only at the instinctual level. Nor need I, I presume, make an argument along the same lines for Mickey Rooney's Puck. No one who has seen the movie needs to be convinced by argument that that is a performance work of art, whatever one thinks of Hollywood's Shakespeare.

What about example (iv), my whistling tunes from *Carmen*? A performance? A performance art work? Don't be absurd. But wait a bit. I am a fairly musical guy; and I whistle with a good deal of musicality and feeling. If the untalented young pianist's product is the limiting case of a performance art work, I think my whistling is a bit beyond that, although I will not press the point.

Finally, example (viii): Julie Harris' out-loud reading of *Jane Eyre*, which has come up before in the discussion. Nothing much more need be added here. Obviously Julie Harris' rendition of *Jane Eyre* is a performance art work of a superior kind, for all of the usual reasons we might give.

So what should we make of all of this? The point is that in deciding which of these doings are at least borderline cases, which *bona fide* but minimal cases, which full-blown cases of performance art works, we simply apply some fairly ordinary, informal, commonsensical criteria. I am not, it is necessary to remind the reader, assuming here any philosophical theory of "what art really is." All that I am doing is employing criteria that perfectly ordinary people, untainted by theory, would adduce, if they were asked in any given instance whether what they had just heard qualified as a performance *work of art*. "Well," I think someone might say, "she did play with feeling; she didn't just 'play the notes,'" or, "It was really a very musical performance for someone so young; there was a real sense of phrasing," and so on. But although this is not, as I have said, intended to imply or favor any theory of art that implied performances, as described above, are art works, I take it that any theory of art that implied that, at least the reasonable candidates, are *not* art works would be, because of that implication alone, an unsatisfactory theory.

But one important point to notice, before we go on to silent readings, is that I think a useful distinction can be made between performances which are, and performances which are not performance art works. The seal's "performance" is not a performance. However, we may want to say that the talentless nine-year-old's product is a performance but not a per-formance art work. On what grounds? I think the grounds are *evaluative* grounds. The criteria applied above in claiming that some of the above examples are not merely performances but performance art works are value criteria. A performance must achieve a certain level of "goodness," *qua* performance, before we are willing to call it a performance art work.

But saying this does not contradict my previous warning that the ques-tion of what an art work is should not be confused with what a *good* art work is. For the value criteria adduced in deciding if a performance qual-ifies as a performance art work are not adduced to distinguish between good and bad performance art works. In other words, a performance can be good enough to be a performance art work; but this says nothing to the question of whether it is a good or bad *performance art work*.

With all of that now on the table, our question is whether it has any bearing on the case in hand, which is to say, silent readings of fictional lit-erature. And here is why I think that it does.

Once we put aside the notion that silent novel and short story readings cannot be performances or performance art works because of their "pecu-liar," silent, private mental existence, then it is fair to suggest, it seems to me, that if such ordinary, unpretentious things as a nine-year-old's piano performance, and the other examples I have adduced, can run the gamut from borderline case of performance art work to full-blown performance art work, then silent readings of literary fiction should as well. If Julie Harris' out-loud reading of *Jane Eyre* counts, uncontroversially, as a performance art work, why shouldn't her silent reading of it to herself, in preparation for her out-loud reading, just as a conductor's silent reading of a score, prior to conducting it, would count as a silent performance? And if a talented nine-year-old's piano performance of a Bach minuet counts as at least a minimal performance art work, why shouldn't my silent reading of a novel?

Silent readings of novels and short stories, then, should be expected to display a wide range of examples, from those so inept, by inept, inexperi-enced readers, that we would not want to countenance them as perform-ance art works at all, to those by readers of experience and taste, that are as much performance art works as silent readings of musical scores by experi-enced and talented musicians of taste and musicality. That, at least, is how the matter appears to me.

And, finally what of claim (c), that readers are just ordinary folks, and artists very unusual, extraordinary individuals, making it absurd to refer to silent readers as "artists"? Well, if you have accepted my defense of per-fectly ordinary, unassuming performance events as performance art works, then it seems to me you are obliged to accept that the perpetrators of these performance events, ordinary and unassuming as they may be, are performance artists, and I will say no more about it.

None of this, needless to say, constitutes a knock-down argument for the art status of (some) silent readings. Many will still find it "very odd" to call the silent readings of novels performances, let alone performance *works of art*. But perhaps what has been said in defense of this "very odd" claim will – I hope it will – give even the serious skeptic some reason to entertain, at least, the *possibility* of their having art status in the ways described above, and that the whole argument of this book will push the claim beyond the merely possible, even for the skeptical reader.

But there are two further problems with the notion of silent readings of fictional literature as performance art works that must give us pause. Let's have a look at them.

20 The Transparency of the Reading Performance

Performances, if indeed they are artworks, as I (and many others) think they are, are themselves objects of artistic appreciation. Thus, when I hear a splendid performance of Beethoven's *Pathétique* Sonata, I am an appreciator not only of Beethoven's work; I am an appreciator, as well, of the *performance*, as a separate (albeit intimately related) artistic object. The problem is that it sounds really weird to suggest that (say) in reading silently to myself *Pride and Prejudice* I am appreciating, enjoying, *both* the novel, *Pride and Prejudice*, and my *reading* of *Pride and Prejudice* as well. There seems no space between them: no way of prising them apart. What could it mean to say that I was both appreciating *Pride and Prejudice* in my reading of it *and* appreciating my *reading* of it?

Let me prelude what I am going to say about this problem with a story, perhaps apocryphal, perhaps not, that may or may not have some relevance here. It is said that Donald Francis Tovey, who was something of a musical prodigy, was discovered one day, as a very young boy, in a room by himself, clapping his hands. When asked what was going on he replied that he had just read to himself in score a string quartet (I think it was), and had become so absorbed that it was as if he were hearing a live performance. It was such a good performance, he said, that, without thinking what he was doing, he quite naturally broke into enthusiastic applause.

I find this story believable; and if it is true it makes the point that, at least in some, albeit unusual circumstances, it does make sense to distinguish, in a silent reading, between appreciation of the work and appreciation of the performance thereof. But that point having been made, I do not want to make too much of it. There is a big difference between a musical prodigy, with abundant musical skills, reading a score, and the ordinary reader of a novel. And if in the former case it does seem plausible to think of the reader appreciating and evaluating the silent performance as a performance, it stretches credulity in the latter. I think what we are tempted, anyway, to say is that except in rare, bizarre, but perhaps possible cases, the performance in silent reading of literary fiction becomes transparent to the reader, as music performance frequently does to the listener, particularly if he or she is not a musician or musically trained, the difference being, of course, that in the case of musical performance, one can, at will, concentrate on the performance per se, whereas in the silent reading of fiction, one might want to say that one hardly knows what it would *mean* to switch one's concentration from work to performance.

Perhaps one can, at times, become self-consciously aware of what one is *doing* when reading silently to oneself. And perhaps that is a case of appreciating one's reading as a work of art. I don't know. But I think the altogether *safe* thing to say, as I have done before, is that it was never my intention to insist on a one-to-one correspondence between every feature of performance, in the conventional performing arts, and every feature of silent reading, in the silently read literary arts. And in the lack of separation of art work from performance art work, in the silently read arts, we may have reached the limit of the analogy.

That being the case – if, that is, the analogy breaks down here – the breakdown can at least be made more philosophically palatable if one can adduce a reason why we should *expect* such a breakdown at this point, thus eliminating the sense of simply, so to say, an *ad hoc* failure of theory. I think such a reason can indeed be adduced.

If we compare the case of the silently read musical score to the case of the silently read work of literary fiction, one glaring and absolutely crucial difference should not escape our vigilance: it is, very simply, the difference between music and *language*. Now whatever the status and significance of music (of some kind or another) to the human species, the status and significance of *language* far outstrips it, on any serious, informed account of either. Whether or not there is agreement on the matter, language has been proposed as one of the things that makes us *human*. Whether or not there is agreement on the matter, language has been proposed as the medium of human thought. Whatever inflated ideas about music the musical enthusiast might entertain, this far, I presume, he will not go.

Furthermore, score-reading is a rare phenomenon, as we have seen. It is, so to speak, historically rare, because the musical score is a very recent arrival in music history. It is geographically rare in that musical notation, of which the score is an instance, is an almost exclusively Western phenomenon. And, finally, it is "demographically" rare in that very very few members of any population possess the mental capacity and training to do the thing. In short, *any* normal human being can acquire the ability to read silently, and very large numbers do. A very very few can or do ever acquire the ability to silently read a musical score and realize thereby a performance in the head.

Taking all of this into account then, it seems no surprise that there should be a marked difference between the experience of silent score-reading and the experience of silently read literary fiction: that if either should be an experience in which the silent performance is transparent to the reader, it should be the one whose medium of expression is so deeply imbedded in the human character as to be "second nature." As might be expected, then, reading to oneself silently, in one's own natural language, is a performance in which it is difficult, and highly unusual, to tell the dancer from the dance.

Be that as it may, there *does* still seem to be some good sense in saying that when one reads a novel silently to onself one is enjoying the *performance*, transparency of performance to the contrary notwithstanding. Here is why.

Consider the sophisticated, musically knowledgeable concert-goer. Such a person would, no doubt be, at times, keenly aware of the performance, *qua* performance and be able to offer, at the end of the concert, comments and opinions about *how* the music was performed.

Contrast such a listener, however, with your average concert-going music-lover, who has neither musical training nor anything above slight, anecdotal knowledge of works, composers, or performers. To *this* listener, I suggest, the musical performance *would* be pretty much transparent. *This* listener would, it might be fair to say, hear the music but not hear the performance, and so would have nothing to tell us about the performance *per se* when asked.

Yet there is a perfectly robust sense in which we *do* want to say that the unsophisticated, non-knowledgeable listener hears the performance. *Of course* he hears the performance. How else could he hear the work? In experiencing the work he is, *eo ipso*, experiencing the performance. That is the way with music (and some other of the performing arts). In experiencing the work you are experiencing the performance; in experiencing the performance you are experiencing the work. The work is present as the performance; the performance is an instance of the work.

Furthermore, and this is the point, the same can be said for novel-reading. In the same sense in which the musical performance is transparent to the unsophisticated, non-knowledgeable music-lover, the reading performance is transparent to most novel readers in most circumstances. In the same sense in which, when the unsophisticated, non-knowledgeable music-lover hears the work, he hears also a performance of the work, the reader, when she "hears" (experiences) the novel, also "hears" (experiences) her "in the head" performance of the novel.

The upshot of the foregoing is that there *is* a robust, full-blooded sense in which the novel reader, like the music listener, experiences the performance of the work as well as the work itself. So if one were worried that the transparency of performance, in novel-reading, makes the claim that novel-reading *is* performance untenable, that worry can now be put aside. There are quite straightforward cases of transparency of performance in music listening, where we still want to say the performance is heard. Thus the transparency of performance in silent novel-reading does not, *of itself,* defeat the reading/performance analogy. To be sure, the notion of *separating,* in one's experience, the performance from the work, in the silent reading of the novel, and concentrating one's attention on the performance alone, may well be misplaced in the novel-reading experience. But it was never my claim that the analogy between musical performance (or poetry performance) and the performance of silent reading must be a *perfect* one. And here perhaps is one place where the analogy may not hold. An analogy, after all, like many other things, can be good without being perfect.

But given what perhaps should be termed the "relative" transparency of silent reading performances, there is this further qualification that ought appropriately to be made. Compare my re-hearing of a piano sonata performed by a pianist other than the one experienced in a previous hearing, and my re-reading of a novel after some years of further literary experiences, both of other literary works and the writings of literary critics.

In my re-hearing of the piano sonata, performed by a different pianist, I would certainly be very much more aware, if I were an attentive listener, of the performance itself, and how it differed from the former one. By parity of reasoning, my re-reading of the novel might well make me more aware, if I were an attentive reader, of the *reading performance itself,* and how *it* differed from the former one, given my changed perspective and increased literary sensibility. Thus, although the "relative" transparency of the silent reading performance seems more or less correct, and the analogy to musical performance strained at this point, we should not allow this to obscure the very real fact that the silent reading performance *can,* at certain crucial times, become an object of consciousness and appreciation much in the way a musical performance does. It is neither a bizarre occurrence nor infrequent to the vanishing point.

21 Read it again, Sam

There is, finally, a possible argument against the notion that silent readings of fictional works are performances of them that can be extracted from a comparison of our attitudes and behavior *vis-à-vis* the re-experiencing of art works already experienced before. Consider the following conversational snippets.

> *Martha.* I have an extra ticket to tonight's performance of the B-minor Mass. Would you like to come?
>
> *Sam.* No thanks. I've heard it.
>
> *Martha.* I have an extra copy of *Pride and Prejudice.* Would you like to have it?
>
> *Sam.* No thanks. I've read it.

Now Sam's response in the first conversation seems altogether nutty. The B-minor Mass is one of those art works that we want to experience over and over again, and were meant to be experienced that way.

But Sam's response in the second conversation is far from being nutty. Indeed, it is quite reasonable. There is nothing at all odd in declining to read a novel one has already read, even if it is a masterpiece like *Pride and Prejudice.* Normally, one tends to read a novel but once.

Why the difference? Why is music a repeatable art and the novel not?

One obvious answer is that we can hear a piece of music over and over again because each time we hear it, although the *music* is the same, the *performance* is different. And it is the difference in performance that makes each experience of the work a *different* experience. Furthermore, if novel-readings were performances, we would re-read novels over and over again, for the same reason we do so with musical works. Therefore, the repeatability of music, and the non-repeatability of novel-reading constitute evidence against the claim that novel-reading is a kind of performance. If it were, we would read novels over and over again, as we hear music over and over again.

However, there is one pretty obvious problem with this argument which can be brought out with another bit of conversation.

> *Martha.* I'm going to the Louvre today. Would you like to come?
>
> *Sam.* No thanks. I've seen those paintings before.

Again, Sam's response is odd, if not nutty. The kinds of masterpieces hanging in the Louvre *are* the kinds of art works we want to, and do experience over and over again. But they are *not* performance works. So the reason we experience *them* over and over again *cannot* be that we see a different performance of the work each time. Repeatability, then, cannot be an argument against the thesis that novel-readings are performances. For performance, clearly, is not a necessary condition for repeatability.

Indeed, even the phenomenon of re-hearing music cannot be entirely explained by the novelty of performance. For many people have only one recording of each work of music in their record collections, yet they listen to their favorite works over and over again, even when it is the *same* performance each time. What this shows is that music-lovers are far more interested in re-experiencing the work than in experiencing different performances of it, even though the latter is certainly *one* important motive for re-hearing.

Furthermore, there is a plausible reason for the non-repeatability of novel-reading that has nothing to do with performance, one way or the other. Probably the over-riding motive for reading novels is to be told a story. And to put it crassly, once you know the story – once you know how things come out – the major source of artistic satisfaction has been exhausted. So if, indeed, the normal reader reads a novel a second time, it will be after a period of time long enough for the general outline as well as the details of the plot to have faded from memory, in effect making it *as if* he or she were experiencing the work for the first time.

But now for an exception that, in the good old-fashioned sense, "proves" the rule, which is to say, tests the above generalization about the tendency not to reread novels and other works of silently read literary fiction. Vladimir Nabokov writes of novel-reading:

> A good reader, a major reader, an active and creative reader is a rereader. And I shall tell you why. When we read a book for the first time the very process of laboriously moving our eye from left to right, line after line, page after page, this complicated physical work upon the book, the very process of learning in terms of space and time what the book is about, this stands between us and artistic appreciation . . .. The element of time does not really enter in a first contact with a painting. In reading a book we must have time to acquaint ourselves with it . . .. But at a second, or third, or fourth reading we do, in a sense, behave towards a book as we do towards a painting.[106]

It seems clear the kind of reading experience Nabokov has in mind: just the kind that would be cultivated by a practicing novelist interested in studying and improving his craft. For it is only in the second or third or fourth reading of a novel that its deep structure and narrative techniques become apparent to us; that we can, as it were, see behind the scenes.

If, of course, this were the way the novel, as a rule, were read, we would indeed have an answer to the objection that since performance works tend to be experienced repeatedly, and novels are not, novels cannot be performance works. The first premise would be false and the argument would fail.

Now it is surely no intent of mine to deny that such novel-reading as Nabokov describes is appropriate and rewarding. But it is not the way most readers enjoy novels, who *do* enjoy them, including the serious ones, the great ones, the works of genius. And so the above argument is of no avail to me.

Nabokov refers to the practitioner of this kind of novel-reading as "A good reader, a major reader, an active and creative reader . . .," with the clear implication that this is the *only* kind of reader that can be so described. But here I think we should dig in our heels and resist the kind of over-intellectualizing of the novel-reading experience that Nabokov is involved in. The kind of reader he describes is certainly not the normal reader, nor is it the reader or kind of reading for which many if not *most* of the great as well as the not-so-great novels were written. They were written for a thinking reader, yes. However, they were written to be read and enjoyed and thought about by folks who read for pleasure, read a novel generally only once, and then move on to something else. "No thanks – read that," or, perhaps, in the other case, "I just reread *The Magic Mountain* – haven't read it since I was an undergraduate: it was as if I were reading it for the first time."

Of course Nabokov's reader is "A good reader, a major reader, an active and creative reader . . ."; but so too, I would like to urge, *can be* the reader of great and serious novels for whom once is enough. They are by far the greater number of the good, major, active and creative readers. And I believe they are the readers for whom the great novels have been primarily written (with well-known exceptions). To give the palm only to the Nabokov-style reader is, it appears to me, to succumb to a very unpleasant form of intellectual snobbery.

The non-repeatability of the novel, then, is, Nabokov's reader to the contrary notwithstanding, the general rule, but, as we have seen, is no argument against silent novel-reading being a kind of performance. Which is not to say, however, that it is a performance in as full-blooded a sense as the musical performance, or that, *qua* performance, it contributes as much to the artistic experience.

22 Silent Soundings and Silent Performances

Having defended, at some length, the notion that silent readings of novels *can be* performances, two important and related questions need now be addressed. They are: Are *all* instances of a novel, all tokens of the type, silent *performance* readings? And, second, are *any* silent readings of non-literary texts silent *performance* readings? The answer to the first of these questions is an obvious "No"; and the answer to the second seems to be a non-obvious "No."

With regard to the first question, the following example will prove helpful.[107] A computer can "sound out" a text. If, for instance, one downloads *Pride and Prejudice*, the computer sounds out a token of the novel. But it is hardly a *performance*. Obviously, the computer has no "interpretation" of the work on which the sounding is based. And the sounding, furthermore, is produced in a mechanical, expressionless monotone. It is beyond a bad performance; it is a *non*-performance. However, I think we *do* want to say that it is an instance of the work, a token of the work-type, from which a notation, which is to say, a written text, can be derived by a copyist, and from which a *performance* reading can be realized. As well, any *silent* reading of a novel that approached the computer sounding in character would, I think, fail to be a *performance* reading. Thus it seems clear that the ontology of silent fiction-reading does not require that all instances are performances, any more than the musical work ontology requires that all instances of a notated musical work, sounded or silent, must be performance instances.

The second question poses more interesting complications. And to begin to simplify it, let us contrast the silent reading of a fictional work, say, *Pride and Prejudice*, with the silent reading of a philosophical text: to take an imposing example, Kant's *Critique of Pure Reason*.

Even someone who has come to accept my thesis that the silent readings of fictional works are, in most instances, silent *performances*, will, I think, find it implausible to suggest that a silent reading of Kant's first *Critique* is a *performance* of *it*, although it seems clear that it is an *instance*. And that seems right to me. But *why* is it right?

The answer that most readily comes to mind is that *Pride and Prejudice* is a work of art, and the *Critique of Pure Reason* most emphatically is not. And surely it stands to reason that texts which *are* works of art would be amenable to performance whereas texts which are not works of art would not be so amenable.

But as reasonable as this answer is, *prima facie*, and, indeed, I *do* think it is reasonable, it immediately raises another question, which is to say: What is it *about* fictional texts being works of art that makes them amenable to silent reading *performance*, where philosophical texts not being art works, are not? And *this* question is not so easily answered. For if it is being works of art that makes fictional literary texts amenable to silent readings that are *performances*, then we must give an account of what it is that makes fictional literary texts works of art if we are to be able to give an answer to the question of why their being works of art makes them so amenable. In other words, we must have in hand a "definition" of "art." But surely providing such a definition, as I have observed before in another context, would be well beyond the purview of the present monograph, even if I had such a definition to offer (which I do not).

There is, however, something useful that can be done, short of providing a dissertation on defining art, in the way of giving at least a plausible, if not final, conclusive reason for the belief that it is literary texts – which is to say, text art works – and not others, such as philosophical texts, that can eventuate in silent readings that are performances. Towards that end I want, briefly, to look at what is without a doubt the most powerful and impressive theory of what art is to come down the pike since Dewey's *Art as Experience*, and Collingwood's *Principles of Art*, in the 1930s. I refer of course to the theory of Arthur Danto's as laid out in his now classic *Transfiguration of the Commonplace*.

In the above mentioned work Danto offers three necessary and, together, sufficient conditions for arthood. (1) Artworks "are about something (or the question of what they are about may legitimately arise)."[108] (2) "[I]t is analytical to the concept of an artwork that there has to be an interpretation."[109] (3) "[W]orks of art, in categorical contrast with mere representations, use the means of representation in a way that is not exhaustively specified when one has exhaustively specified what is being represented."[110] We shall be paying special attention to condition (3) for reasons that will become apparent in a moment.

The purpose of condition (3), in Danto's scheme, is to distinguish art works from other entities – for example, philosophical texts – that fulfill the first two requirements for arthood. And to put the argument in its most succinct and general form, in art works, *medium matters*. It can never be "transparent," which is to say, absent from consciousness or perceptual awareness, for "an artwork expresses something about its content," through its medium, through its way of representing or expressing its content; and this is "in contrast with an ordinary representation."[111] "The medium toward which the transparency theory has taken so prudish a stance as to pretend that it does not exist and to hope for an illusion through which it will be rendered invisible, is of course never really eliminable."[112]

Furthermore, it is the medium through which we perceive the artist's "style" – what makes her artwork uniquely *hers*. "What would have been transparent to Giotto's contemporaries, almost like a glass they were seeing through to a sacred reality, has become opaque to us, and we are instantly conscious of something invisible to them but precious to us – Giotto's style . . .."[113] Hence the medium, the mode of representation, whether in a work of the visual arts or a work of literary fiction, is, in a way, the "voice" of the artist. "It is as if a work of art were like an externalization of the artist's consciousness, as if we could see his way of seeing and not merely what he saw."[114]

Now I want to suggest that it is just this third condition on arthood that is crucial, if indeed not the whole explanation for what makes the silent readings of literary texts such as *Pride and Prejudice* possible as *performance* readings and the silent readings of philosophical works such as Kant's first *Critique* not. For therein lie the features of literary texts on which performance most relies. A performance, as opposed to a mere sounding, gives voice not merely to the "content" of the literary work but to the "tone of voice" of its creator and/or narrator. It is in the medium, in the mode of representation or expression that the performance finds its distinctive materials. It is because, in literary texts, and not in philosophical texts, the medium "says" something about its content, that it is realizable in a silent *performance*; it is the silent *performance* that realizes the "aboutness" not only of the content but of the medium – and *especially* of *that*. To a philosophical text such as the *Critique of Pure Reason*, the medium is irrelevant; and that is why, in theory at least, its full content can be realized in translation or paraphrase. To a work of literary art, the medium is essential, for the reasons stated above, and the aspect of it that makes it "performable." That at least is my hypothesis.

Now it will not have escaped the vigilant reader that there *are* philosophical texts not only amenable to performance, but actually intended for it, namely the Socratic dialogues of Plato. But this surely is no real counterexample. For these dialogues are generally acknowledged to be literary, which is to say artistic masterpieces. They are at once philosophical texts and transcendent works of art. As has often been pointed out by interpreters, their medium, which is to say their dialogue form, is, as it were "part" of their philosophical content. The philosophical dialogue is, of course, a genre that has endured; and it runs the gamut from the rather wooden ones of Bishop Berkeley, say, with their abstract characterless discussants, Hylas, Philonous, Alciphron, and their ilk, to the literary masterpieces of

Plato. But even the former provide some purchase for performance, and are at least minimal works of art, if limiting cases. So the fact that some philosophical texts are performable need not trouble us. It is, obviously, no paradox to say that *some* philosophical texts are, as well, literary texts, which is to say, artworks.

A more serious objection to what I have been claiming here is that my answer to the question of why novels are silently performable and such things as philosophical texts are not depends upon the correctness of Danto's definition of art. But such definitions, the objection will go on, are highly controversial, and there are numerous of them out there on offer.

My response is that I have based my conjecture solely on the third condition of Danto's definition. And it appears to me that whatever may be the final verdict on Danto's definition of art as a whole, the third condition will stand. Or, to put it another way, any *other* definition of art that is in the running must do adequate justice to the nature and role of the artistic medium as Danto has so insightfully presented it. On *its* validity, not on the validity of Danto's definition *tout court*, I am willing to rely in my account of the difference between silently performable and nonperformable texts.

At this juncture it is time to press on, and turn in another direction, or, rather to turn back in a direction in which we have already gone. I want, in fact, to return, now, to Ion for another look. He still has much to teach us.

23 The Other Ion

Part of what Ion does seems perfectly reasonable to us; the other part seems very strange (at least to me). It is the strange part that I want to consider seriously now.

Let me begin by reminding the reader that *each* of Plato's depictions of the reciter of poetry, the one in *Ion*, and the one in *Republic* III, ascribes to that character something strange. Both characters, of course, recite poetry; there is nothing strange to us in that. Poetry recitation is still part of our literary art world, as it was of Plato's.

What is strange to us about the narrative performer described in the *Republic* is his propensity for "imitating" non-human sounds. You will recall that Plato says of him: "he will be ready to imitate anything . . . . [H]e will attempt to represent the roll of thunder, the noise of wind and hail, or the creaking of wheels, and pulleys, and the various sounds of flutes, pipes, trumpets, and all sorts of instruments: he will bark like a dog, bleat like a sheep, or crow like a cock . . .," and so on. Plato's contempt for this character is quite outspoken: he is, in a word, "unscrupulous," and, I am tempted to add, "vulgar."[115] And it is hard for us to imagine exactly what kind of performance this character gave. It is not like anything we know in our own art world, except, perhaps, a recitation for children. (I remember that my mother used to imitate the sound of the wind when she read to me one of the episodes in *Winnie the Pooh*.)

Ion the rhapsode, as we have seen, is also regarded in a negative light by Plato. But it is with a gentle humor and mild irony that Plato represents him, not the undisguised contempt that characterizes his representation of the narrative performer in the *Republic*. Whatever his pretensions, Ion has a certain dignity, and is devoted, heart and soul, to the greatest of the Greek poets. It is difficult to think of him interlarding his performance with the bleating of sheep. So I think it reasonable to suppose that Ion is likely not to be identified with the "unscrupulous" performer in *Republic* III. He is obviously a more up-scale performer: he does not ply his trade on street corners or play to the groundlings.

What we find strange about Ion's performance is that he interlards it, as we have seen, with what we would call "critical commentary." The closest I suppose we come is the "poetry reading," where the author tells us something about her poem, and then reads it. But Ion, after all, is reciting narration, and, apparently, interrupting the story to comment on it. There seems to be nothing like that in our experience of the arts. (Perhaps there is in places where oral traditions of story telling still linger on.)

Now one strategy I might employ at this juncture is to simply reject this aspect of Ion's performance as irrelevant to my picture of the silent reader of fiction. Why not simply say that what we represent in playing our roles, in silent reading, is Ion the teller of tales, not Ion the critic? The latter function for us is performed by a different person, through a different experience.

I do not follow this obvious course because, contrary to what might first appear, I think, as I said early on, Ion's function as critical commentator, during his performance, has something important to tell us about silent reading. It is not just a dead practice of the ancient Greek literary experience but, when properly viewed, in the modern context, a living practice of our own literary experience. Even through Plato's jaundiced eye, Ion still has something more to teach us about what is happening when we read novels to ourselves.

First, we must try to conjecture, from only the most meager hints on Plato's part, what Ion was really doing in his capacity of commentator-in-performance.

As we saw when I first introduced Ion to the reader, the rhapsode describes himself, somewhat immodestly, as "being able to speak about Homer better than any man . . .." And he continues, in this vein, to aver that no "one else who ever was, had as good ideas about Homer as I have, or as many."[116] The question is, what is it in Homer that Ion speaks about? What is the content of the many good ideas Ion comes up with anent the *Iliad* and *Odyssey*?

What seems abundantly clear, both from what Plato says in the *Ion*, and in the *Republic* as well, is that Ion the rhapsode speaks, we would say, about the "content," not the "form" or "style" of Homeric poetry. He speaks about what Homer *means*: he is an interpreter of the subject matter.

Now we must be careful about what we infer here. Plato was violently opposed to the use the Greek citizenry made of the content of the Homeric poems: the content about which Ion spoke. So we certainly are not getting, here, a disinterested account. Furthermore, it does not follow that even if the Greeks misused the content of the poems in the way Plato averred, that *we* must misuse it in that way. *A fortiori*, it does not follow that if the Greeks misused this content, the content has no proper use. With these cautionary precepts in mind, let's see what we *can* learn from Plato about what Ion said.

Let us start with what Plato says Homer said:

> Does not Homer speak of the same themes which all other poets handle? Is not war his greatest argument? And does he not speak of human society and of intercourse of men, good and bad, skilled and unskilled, and of the gods conversing with one another and with mankind, and about what happens in heaven and in the world below, and the generations of gods and heroes? Are these the themes of which Homer sings?[117]

Homer, and all of the other poets speak, then, of the same things; and what they speak of, which is what raises Plato's hackles, are all things that involve specialized skills or crafts or knowledge: in other words, subjects better left to experts in these skills or crafts or branches of learning. War should be left to the generals to speak about, but Homer speaks about war. The nature of the gods should be left to the priests and prophets to speak about, but Homer speaks about the nature of the gods. And so on.

Ion speaks about what Homer speaks about. Or, more precisely, Ion makes clear to his listeners what Homer is saying about his subjects: war and theology and the rest: "interpretation," Ion insists, "has certainly been the most laborious part of my art."[118] But that is not all. Ion also expresses opinions of his own about the content of what Homer has said, and Ion interpreted, at least to the extent that he judges whether Homer's words have been *appropriate* or not to the subject matter in question. We know this because Plato upbraids him for it. The well-known Platonic dictum is that "he who has no knowledge of a particular art will have no right judgement of the sayings and doings of that art." And so the answer elicited from Ion to Socrates' question, "Then which will be a better judge of the lines [about chariot-driving] which you were reciting from Homer, you or the charioteer?," is "The charioteer."[119]

The evaluation of Plato's frequently disturbing critical comments on poetry is not my subject, nor am I qualified to make it my subject. All I wish to extract from these comments is the conclusion that Ion the rhapsode, whether justifiably or not, not only interpreted the poems he recited to his audience, as part of his performance, but expressed opinions about the truth or falsity, appropriateness or inappropriateness of what the poets were saying as well. In other words, Ion the rhapsode thought about the content of what he was reciting and expressed these thoughts to his listeners as part of his recitation. Ion was clearly treating the Homeric poems as a potential source of knowledge and was, as part of his performance, commenting upon the validity or invalidity of these claims to his audience. He was, one might say, "thinking out loud."

One is tempted to think of Ion, in his role of commentator on the content of the Homeric poems, as playing something like the role of the chorus in the tragedies. And his "strangeness," in this regard, to the modern reader, may well be analogous to the "strangeness" a modern audience experiences in the theatre, when the tragic chorus makes *its* pronouncements on the dramatic proceedings. It is, I suppose, one of the principal challenges to the modern director of Greek tragedy to make the chorus "fit in" to the play as the modern audience expects it to: which is to say, as part of the dramatis personae.

One of the familiar ways of looking at the evolution of the chorus in Greek tragedy, from Aeschylus to Euripides, is as an evolution from what might be thought of as an "external commentator" on the proceedings to a character or characters in the drama. As an external commentator, the chorus, it seems to me, might serve somewhat the same purpose I imagine Ion serves in his role as commentator on the content of the Homeric epic: it is an initiator of thought in the audience about what moral, philosophical, or other propositions the author means to convey by his work. This seems to me very much like the role the chorus plays, for example, in Aeschylus' *Eumenides*, where it is so obvious that "philosophical" and "moral" issues are meant to be raised and thought about.

If Ion is his own "Greek chorus," then he has a direct historical precedent in the chorus of Aeschylian tragedy, which is perhaps why a Greek audience found this aspect of the rhapsode's performance (as I presume it did) familiar and unremarkable even though the chorus no longer exhibited it in the plays of Sophocles and Euripides.

Do we have room for *this* Ion in our literary experience? I think that we do. But before I try to make room in my account for what, after all, seems a very odd aspect indeed of Ion's activity as performer, I think it is necessary to explore the possibility that I have misinterpreted Plato, in regard to it, and that what he is ascribing to Ion is really something quite apart from performance altogether.[120]

I have envisaged Ion's performance of the Homeric epics as one in which he both recites the poetry and, at times, comments on its meaning, that is to say, "interprets" it as a literary critic might do. This would, as is obvious, make it a strange kind of performance according to modern sensibilities. There are, however, other possible ways of construing what Plato is saying that make Ion's activities as "critic" far less peculiar; and they need to be considered.

To start with, it is clear that Ion sometimes talks about Homer in ordinary conversation, as he is doing in the dialogue; and there is nothing odd in that, nor is it part of his performance as rhapsode. He is "talking shop."

Furthermore, Ion is represented by Plato as responding to the performances of other rhapsodes with comments about Homer of what we might call a critical kind, where he has Socrates say: "you . . . are possessed by Homer; and when any one repeats the words of another poet you go to sleep, and know not what to say; but when any one recites a strain of Homer you wake up in a moment, and your soul leaps within you, and you have plenty to say [about Homer]."[121] It is not clear just what the circumstances are under which Ion hears and comments on the performances of his rivals. Was there an "official" time for such in the context of the performance? Or are these responses of Ion's to informal presentations? Rehearsals perhaps? In any case, they are not part of Ion's performances, and pose no particular problem for our comprehension.

However, I think it is clear enough from the text, although not, perhaps, completely beyond doubt, that Ion not only talked about Homer in the informal ways described above but in public performance as well. As I say, I cannot put this claim beyond all doubt, but it does seem to me that the tenor of some of the remarks Plato puts in Socrates' mouth strongly suggests it.

Consider the following exchange:

Socrates. I often envy the profession of a rhapsode, Ion; for you have always to wear fine clothes, and to look as beautiful as you can is a part of your art. Then, again, you are obliged to be continually in the company of many good poets; and especially Homer, who is the best and most divine of them; and to understand him, and not merely learn his words by rote, is a thing greatly to be envied . . ..

Ion. Very true, Socrates; interpretation has certainly been the most laborious part of my art; and I believe myself able to speak about Homer better than any man; and that neither Metrodorus of Lampsacus, nor Stesimbrotus of Thasos, nor Glaucon, nor any one else who ever was, had as good ideas about Homer as I have, or as many

Socrates. I am glad to hear you say so, Ion; I see that you will not refuse to acquaint me with them.

Ion. Certainly, Socrates; and you really ought to hear how exquisitely I [embellish] Homer. I think that the Homeridae should give me a golden crown.

Socrates. I shall take an opportunity of hearing your embellishments of him at some other time . . ..[122]

The first point I want to make about this snippet of conversation is that it puts almost beyond doubt that Ion gives formal presentations not only of Homer's poetry but of his views on the meaning of the poetry, which is to say, his interpretations of it. Ion the rhapsode, as Socrates says, dresses up and looks as fine as he can, and then, as Ion says, he goes on to talk about Homer better than anyone else. Surely this implies a public performance in which Ion expresses his ideas about Homer. (You don't have to dress up to express them informally to Socrates in the Agora.)

This of course still leaves open the possibility that Ion gave two different kinds of performance, on separate occasions, one in which he recited Homer, the other in which he talked about him as in a public lecture (of which more in a moment). And I don't think that this possibility can be entirely ruled out by the text. But I find the text more strongly suggestive of the idea that Ion's performances were "mixed": that he recited Homer and talked about him in the *very same* performance. Here is why.

First of all, in the passage quoted, and in the dialogue as a whole, Ion's ability to recite Homer and his ability to talk about and praise him always seem mushed together, always mentioned in the same breath. There is never an attempt to disambiguate them or suggest that they take place on separate formal occasions.

But second, and more conclusive still, are these words of Ion's in the passage quoted above: "you really ought to hear how exquisitely I [embellish] Homer."

In his performance of Homer, then – that is to say, in his recitation of Homer's poetry – Ion embellishes the poetry. What does he embellish it with? What has just gone before tells us unequivocally: he embellishes it with his comments about Homer which, he immodestly tells us, are better than anyone else's, living or dead. Clearly, then, it would seem Ion both recites Homer and talks about him in the same performance; for the comments about Homer are embellishments to his recitation of the poetry. It is for this total performance, Homer cum interpretational embellishments, that he feels entitled to the golden crown of the Homeridae, the Sons of Homer, and for which he won first prize at the festival of Asclepius in Epidaurus, from where, we are told at the outset of the dialogue, he has just returned.

But now for an opinion completely different alluded to a moment ago, and worthy of serious consideration because of its authoritative source.

The translator of the Loeb Classical Library *Ion*, W. R. M. Lamb, writes in his Introduction: "The 'rhapsode,' Ion of Ephesus, appears before us in the two capacities of reciter and expositor of Homer." And he adds, later on: "But besides these public recitals they [the rhapsodes] gave lectures on the subject matter of the poems to classes of those who hoped to acquire some practical knowledge from their interpretations and disquisitions . . .."[123] Thus, if Lamb is to be credited, Ion and his ilk gave two kinds of "performances" in separate venues: recitations of poetry and "classes" on its meaning.

To my eye Plato's *Ion* paints a different picture, as I have tried to show. But perhaps historical scholarship should prevail over a philosophical text perceived through the lens of personal interpretation, particularly as it is the lens of a Greekless reader, clouded by translation. In any case, as will become apparent later on, it does not much matter to the use to which I will put Ion's second "performance," as expositor of Homer, whether it is part of his recital of Homer or a separate "recital," or (perhaps?) both. So the reader may choose, as he or she wishes, between my impressionistic understanding of Plato's text, and Lamb's more prosaic, but mayhap historically more accurate one, without rejecting the philosophical point about the modern silent reading of literary texts to come, based on Ion's dual occupation of reciter and expositor.

Now there are two perfectly rational responses at this point. One might find the notion of a poetry recital embellished with comments on the poetry so bizarre and improbable as to render my interpretation of the text, to the contrary notwithstanding, off the mark in some way yet to be determined. Or one can accept that the Greeks of Plato's age had a way of doing this business that was radically different from our own but yet neither bizarre nor improbable if, perhaps, we can understand it to have analogies in our own literary practices. It is the latter approach that I take in what follows. However, the reader who favors the former alternative, and perhaps wishes to follow Lamb's alternative can, with some minor adjustments, make my ensuing remarks consistent with it. I will leave it to that reader to make them unaided.

So my task now is to show that we do indeed have room for *my* peculiar Ion in contemporary literary practice, in particular, of course, in the practice of silently read fiction. But showing it requires going off at what might appear to be something of a tangent that involves propounding and defending a certain "theory" of fictional literature. That theory is sometimes called the propositional theory of literary truth and is, I take it, part of a truth theory of literary value. I shall be outlining and partially defending this theory in the following five sections, after which we can return to the "other Ion" and work him into the equation.[124]

24 Literature and Truth

The propositional theory of truth says that the purpose of literary works is to express propositions, frequently, but not solely of a philosophical or moral character, which are offered up as veridical. The truth theory of literary value says that a literary work is of high literary value to the extent to which these expressed propositions *are* veridical, of low literary value to the extent to which they are not. And the objection to this bipartite theory I want to respond to is that, in general, the propositions that defenders of the theory extract from great literary works are so banal, so trivial as to be impotent to bestow any palpable value on the works that express them, even when true – hence cannot possibly account for the high literary value of such works.

The first refinement I must put on this general statement of the proposed argument is to greatly reduce the scope of the propositional theory of literature. The version I wish to defend merely says that *part* of the purpose of *some*, but by no means *all* literary works is the expression of true propositions.

The second refinement is to greatly reduce the scope of the truth theory of literary value which, clearly, is made necessary not only by the reducing in scope of the propositional theory, but by ordinary philosophical prudence as well. Because the expression of propositions is neither the sole purpose of *any* literary work nor a purpose at all of *many* literary works, the value of literary works *tout court* cannot possibly rest solely on truth and falsity. Rather, we want to say that *one* of the good-making features of *some* literary works is that the propositions they express are true, and *one* of the bad-making features of *some* works is that the propositions they express are false.

A word now must be said about the scope of the phrase "literary work," and the ways in which literary works "express" propositions. Right now I am taking the concept of literature and literary work rather broadly, to include not merely fictional works like plays, novels, and narrative poems, but non-fictional works, such as didactic poetry, philosophical poems, and lyric poetry as well. I do so because, from antiquity until the development of the modern novel, and modern reading habits, philosophers and critics have done the same, and I think we can learn something relevant to present concerns from that. But I do want to emphasize that fictional works will be, unless otherwise apparent from the context, uppermost in my mind, as they have been throughout these pages. For they are the controversial cases. It is easy to see that and how Lucretius' *De Rerum Natura*, Horace's *Ars Poetica*, or Pope's *Essay on Man* express propositions, and why one might want to say that that is an essential part of the exercise in these cases, less easy for *War and Peace* or *Hamlet*.

This brings me to the question of *how* literary works express propositions. Following Peter Lamarque and Stein Olsen, in their important work, *Truth, Fiction, and Literature*, I shall say that a literary work can express propositions either directly or indirectly: stated outright or "implied" (in some non-formal sense of that latter term).[125] Thus, Lucretius' great poem, on my reading of it, anyway, expresses directly, just as the works of Kant and Hume do, propositions about human nature and the nature of the world, whereas Dostoyevsky's novels do so not directly, for the most part; rather, indirectly, by implication or suggestion. In what follows I will assume that everything I say about the propositions that literary works express concerns fictional literature, and indirect expression, but assume, also, that everything I say, if true, is true *a fortiori*, of non-fictional works and direct expression of propositions.

I must now say a word about truth, although the secret of what it is, you may be sure, is safe with me. For, to be perfectly accurate about it, I am not really defending, even in a modest way, a theory of literary truth but, rather, what might, I suppose, be called a theory of literary *plausibility*. Let me explain.

William James, in perhaps his best-known essay, "The Will to Believe," introduced a distinction between what he called "live" and "dead" hypotheses. A live hypothesis is one that appears to the person who contemplates it as at least a viable candidate for belief, even though he or she might not presently believe it. A dead hypothesis, on the other hand, is one that has no such appeal at all, but is taken to be not a possible option, that is to say, not possibly true.[126] In my version, the truth theory of literary value is not the theory that states that expression of true hypotheses is a good-making feature, expression of false hypotheses a bad-making one; rather it is the theory that expression of live hypotheses is a good-making feature, the expression of dead hypotheses a bad-making one. But, I should add, the considerations on the part of the reader or spectator, as to whether an expressed hypothesis is true or false, are part of the literary experience, *both* because such conditions are necessary in determining whether a hypothesis is living or dead, as well as because, so I shall argue later on, it is *part* of the purpose of *some* literary works to get us to think about whether the hypotheses they express, if they are live ones for the reader or spectator, are true or false.

One further general comment on the hypotheses expressed by literary works, before I get on with other matters. I said that, according to what I guess I should now call the plausibility theory of literary value, it is a good-making feature of a literary work that it expresses a live hypothesis as part of its purpose, a bad-making feature if it expresses a dead one. But liveness and deadness are not the only value-considerations with regard to hypotheses. Content also counts, and I have, as yet, said nothing at all about that. Simply put, what needs to be said is that for the expression of a live hypothesis to have any palpable literary value, it must be a hypothesis about something that deeply matters to us. "Perennial themes" are what Lamarque and Olsen call such hypotheses.

Now this stipulation, that the hypotheses that bestow palpable value on literary works expressing them must be important, deeply significant ones, may strike you as in direct conflict with the objection I want to try to deal with here. For the objection is that the hypotheses extracted from the literary works said to express them are too banal to be taken seriously as bestowers of value. But if these hypotheses, when value bestowing, are stipulated by me to be important, deeply significant ones, I am contradicting right from the start the objection I am supposed to be assuming here. Either there *is* no objection, or I am begging the question against it.

The problem, however, is only apparent, being generated by an equivocation. Two senses of "banal" are involved here, in the claim that the hypotheses expressed by literary works, in order to bestow value, must be both live and of deep concern, therefore *not* banal, and the objection that these same hypotheses always turn out to *be* banal. I shall, later on, resolve this apparent tension. For now let it stand with a promissory note in need of redemption.

It will not have escaped your notice, perhaps, that in placing some, although by no means all literary value in the liveness of expressed hypotheses, and in the significance of their content, I have, to some extent, relativized literary value. For what is a live hypothesis to one group of people may well not be for another. The passage of time, the advancement of learning, and many other factors are to blame for that.

Whether anyone will be shocked by this result I do not know. But it certainly coincides with some of our pre-systematic beliefs about value in general, and artistic value in particular. For certainly no one thinks that how we value literary works remains fixed over time – the fact that the canon changes being ample evidence that it does not. Now whether works gain and lose value, or whether their value is constant, and sometimes we get it right, sometimes wrong, is a nice question. I will not try to answer it here, except to say that if one thinks there are perennial themes, deep philosophical and moral theses that have *always* been of major concern to all human beings, and have remained living options for everyone, which may not be an unreasonable thing to claim, then there may be some literary values, according to the proposition theory of literary plausibility, that are permanent, enduring values.

At this point let me summarize what is to come. I want to defend a version of what is called the proposition theory of literary truth, which I will call, rather, the proposition theory of literary plausibility. In defending it, I will also be defending the truth theory of literary value, which I will call, to be consistent with my re-naming of the proposition theory of literary truth, the plausibility theory of literary value. In effect, I will be defending the two-part theory that *one* of the purposes of *some* literary works is to express propositions, frequently moral or, broadly speaking, philosophical ones, which present to us live hypotheses concerning matters of deep and abiding significance. When a literary work succeeds in doing this, it possesses thereby literary value, which I might as well call propositional value. This is by no means the only kind of literary value it possesses, and many literary works do not possess propositional value at all. Propositional value is neither a sufficient nor a necessary condition for a literary work's being a good or a great work of art. It is just one value among many that a literary work might possess.

I am, then, going to defend the proposition theory of literary plausibility, and, in consequence, the plausibility theory of literary value. But my defense is *specific*. I will be defending them against the charge that the propositions advocates of this view extract from literary works are too banal to be any part of their purpose to express, or any part of their value. I will deal with some related objections as well. But the charge of banality is my main target, and its relevance to the main argument of this study will later become apparent. I must begin my defense by stating the objection in more detail.

25 The Banality of Literary Truth

Perhaps the best way to present the banality objection is to produce a sample proposition that has been identified as being expressed by some great literary works and, in relation to them, see what the charge of banality amounts to. I will take a fairly obvious one. Certainly many literary works have expressed it.

Many literary works have, I take it, expressed propositions that center around the issue of freedom and determinism. Some have implied the proposition that determinism is true, some the proposition that there is human freedom (supposing the two to be incompatible).

But surely it needs no ghost come from the grave to tell us these things. They are utter philosophical banalities. That's the point.

Now, clearly, the problem of determinism and free will *is* a problem of deep concern to people. And for most people determinism and free will are live hypotheses, which, of course, is why they are seen as constituting a form of philosophical dilemma.

So the freedom/determinism pair satisfies our previously stipulated requirement that for an expressed hypothesis to bestow value on the work expressing it it must be both live and important. How, then, can it be *banal* as well?

The answer is that it is *philosophically* banal just because everyone who has an acquaintance with philosophy has been acquainted with the problem of free will and determinism since philosophical babyhood. What would make it philosophically *un*banal, philosophically interesting would be a novel *defense* of one or the other hypothesis, or a novel defense of their compatibility – or, if not novel, then more thorough and convincing than previous ones. What makes Kant's or Hume's statement of the freedom/determinism issue interesting rather than banal is that each provides a deep and/or original analysis and defense of compatibilism. But that's the problem. Argument and analysis are not the stuff of literary works, at least the fictional kind, which are, it will be recalled, the crucial kind for anyone desiring to make out a case for the propositional theory of literary plausibility and the plausibility theory of literary value.

Thus, what the defender of these theories must show is how such philosophical hypotheses as "Determinism is true," "Determinism is false,"

"There is no human freedom," or "Compatibilism is true" can escape the charge of banality, when expressed in literary works, where what makes them philosophically interesting in philosophical works, namely analysis and argument, are absent.

To begin with, it is important not to overstate the case for banality by suggesting that the "familiar" philosophical and moral hypotheses expressed by literary works are familiar to *everyone*. The banality thesis is usually put forward by academics – philosophers and literary theorists – to whom these hypotheses *are* "old hat." And we should perhaps remind ourselves that they are not the only audience, indeed not the principal audience at which our great literary works were aimed. To underscore this it might be useful to take a look, again, at the "institution" of literature in some historical perspective.

What I would like to remind you of is that in the ancient world, it was customary to propagate knowledge "at the cutting edge" – philosophical, moral, cosmological, "scientific" – in poetic form. The pre-Socratics, Empedocles and Parmenides, for example, both expressed their world-views in poems (now of course available to us only in isolated fragments); and although Lucretius was, in large part, expressing the world-view of others, which he shared but did not originate, he expressed it in literary form. Literature and knowledge, literature and truth were not, in those times, sundered.

Nor, as we know, was poetic "fiction" thought separated off from philosophical, cosmological or moral knowledge in the ancient world, much to Plato's dismay. There may have been, as Plato said, an ancient quarrel between poetry and philosophy; but there was an ancient alliance as well. Poets were "seers," and therefore were purveyors of knowledge, whether in a "philosophical" poem like Parmenides' *Way of Truth*, or in narrative ones like the *Iliad* and *Odyssey*.

I do not pretend to know why poetry was a standard mode of philosophical expression in the ancient world but not in the modern one. Obviously, it has to do with the comparatively small number of people, in ancient times, who could read at all, all in the "educated," leisured class, the growth of science, scholarship and specialization, the dissemination of the printed word, a middle class, increasing literacy in the modern era – and, I presume, much much more, including, one supposes, the necessity for reading aloud. But the institution of literature is an unbroken tradition for us from Homer and Parmenides to the modern novel.

Now it would clearly be committing the genetic fallacy to argue that because there was an ancient alliance between poetry and philosophy, and an unbroken tradition of literature from then till now, there must *still* be such an alliance. But I think the ancient alliance and the sustaining tradition are at least evidence in favor of the notion that, to some degree anyway, that alliance is still in place. So I am much inclined to share the sentiments of Martha Nussbaum, when she writes that

> After reading Derrida, and not Derrida alone, I feel a certain hunger for blood; for, that is, writing about literature that talks of human lives and choices as if they matter to us.
>
> This is, after all, the spirit in which much great literature has been and is written and read. We do approach literature for play and delight, for the exhilaration of following the dance form and unraveling webs of textual connection . . .. But one of the things that makes literature something deeper and more central for us than a complex game . . . is that it . . . speaks *about us*, about our lives and choices and emotions, about our social existence and the totality of our connections.[127]

But if the alliance between poetry and philosophy, or, more broadly speaking, the alliance between literature and knowledge, remains in place, it clearly does not remain unchanged. In particular, it is not customary to present philosophy, or cosmology, or science, at the cutting edge, in literary form. And so philosophers and cosmologists and scientists do not read novels, or attend plays, with the intention of advancing their particular specialties.

What I would like to emphasize at this point, however, is that novels and plays are not written solely for philosophers, and other specialists. They, even the serious and great ones, are written for a general, educated public that did not exist in the ancient world, or for that matter, until the eighteenth century. And for those folks a play or novel may very well be the place where determinism and freedom of the will, the problem of evil, or the counter-examples to utilitarianism as a moral theory are first encountered. So we are well advised to ask, when we are told that the philosophical or moral hypotheses expressed in literary works are banal because "old hat," "Old hat to *whom*?" In this respect literature remains, as it was in the ancient world, the educator of mankind.

But merely to point out, important though it may be, that the "old hat" conception of the banality of moral and philosophical hypotheses expressed by literary works is, really, an academic objection that touches academics alone, is not enough, I think, to redeem these hypotheses from the charge of "banality" in the deeper sense of lacking the careful analysis and argumentation one has a right to expect in serious philosophical discussion. What further can be said?

As a delaying action, one can point out, I suppose, that literary works are not totally without argument and analysis. Examples like the Grand Inquisitor Sequence in *The Brothers Karamazov*, or the extensive discussions between Naphta and Settembrini in *The Magic Mountain* immediately come to mind. I don't think such examples should be underestimated, either in frequency or in importance. But alone I do not think they can sustain the claim of literature to philosophical and moral depth. They should be added to the sum. They will not, however, tip the scales.

The mandated philosophical move at this point is to claim that literary works, particularly works of fiction, possess methods for accomplishing the same goals that analysis and argument do in standard philosophical and moral discourse, which is to say, clarification and rational justification. Professor Nussbaum has tenaciously pursued one such method, which she describes in two claims: "the claim that there is with respect to any text carefully written and fully imaged, an organic connection between its form and content"; and the "claim . . . that certain truths about human life can only be fittingly and accurately stated in the language and forms characteristic of the narrative artist."[128] I shall say no more about this strategy except that Professor Nussbaum has employed it with considerable skill and ingenuity. I want to pursue another.

26 Gaps and the Afterlife

In the book by Lamarque and Olsen, which I mentioned before, they present the following objection to the propositional theory of literary truth. "The issues of literary criticism," they say, "concern aspects of literary works, and among these issues will be their handling of certain types of themes and concepts, but there is no accepted place for debate about the truth or falsity of general statements about human life or the human condition,"[129] the underlying premise being that *if* it *were* a purpose of literary works to express such propositions as candidates for acceptance or rejection by the reader, debate, in the critical literature about their truth or falsity would be a prominent feature. For, as Lamarque and Olsen add, "The lack of debate in literary criticism and critical discourse in general about the truth of such general propositions must therefore be understood as a feature of the literary practice itself."[130]

But if there is no argument for the philosophical and moral hypotheses expressed by literary works, either in the works themselves or in the critical and interpretive writings about them, it does seem as if they are easy prey to the charge of banality, in just the sense we are now considering. They lack any of the accompanying philosophical debate that makes them live and live again in the philosophical literature: the new interpretation and novel argumentation that renews our interest in them. Suppose, however, as I have suggested elsewhere, the place in literary practice for analysis and argument is neither the literary work nor the critical work: rather, the mind of the reader herself.[131] Let me worry that for a moment.

If one compares the experience of reading a serious novel with the experience of listening to a serious musical work, say, a symphony of Beethoven's, where the reader is a member of the general public, not an "expert," in other words, the reader I have sketched above, we might, with some justice, describe the former, the literary experience, as "gappy" and "sloppy," the latter, the musical experience, as relatively "self-contained." Here is what I mean. In reading a novel of even moderate length, one picks it up, puts it down, picks it up again, without any feeling of narrative discontinuity.[132] Furthermore, the literary experience has what might be compared to the aftertaste of a fine wine, although considerably longer in duration. Call it the "afterlife" of the reading. It is a period subsequent to the completion of the novel during which the images and content linger on in the mind to be savored and thought about. A literary experience, where it is of a serious novel, that lacks this postpartum period of contemplation, lacks something that is, I suggest, an integral part of the full literary experience. Serious novels, then, have a sloppy outer boundary.

Both the gappiness and the sloppiness of the novelistic experience are in sharp contrast to the self-containedness of the musical one. A musical work, such as the usual four-movement symphony, is not meant to be heard, movement by movement, like the chapters of a novel, with, perhaps, wide intervals in between, nor, for most of us, does it have any palpable afterlife; for few music-lovers have either the musical memory, or the musical training (as we have seen) to hear any significant part of a complex musical score in the head.

What I want to suggest, then, is that in the gaps and afterlife of the literary experience, the reader is meant to, among other things, mull over and consider the truth and falsity of those live hypotheses that the novel expresses, as part of its artistic effect. A recent writer has captured my meaning exactly when he describes a moral dilemma raised by Claudio Monteverdi's opera *L'incoronazione di Poppea* as intended "to be debated in the inner academy of the mind."[133] The reader, I suggest, is meant to reason over the hypotheses that serious works of literary fiction present to him for acceptance or rejection; and it is in so doing that these hypotheses gain the depth and breadth for us that lifts them from banality.

Nor is this merely a philosopher's pipe dream – a philosopher's invention to create a "fact" to suit a theory. The notion that we are meant to think, in serous fictional literature, about serious questions and theses which it may pose, that this not only is part of the literary experience of a work, but outlives the reading of it, and that a work's worth is increased by its ability to stimulate such thought, are deeply imbedded in our literary discourse, not just among scholars, but in the general literary community. And I can find no stronger evidence of this claim than the following advertising blurb, quoted from the popular press, on a novel recently read: "Much of the pleasure of reading Chaim Potok's books comes from the fact that he poses questions that remain the subjects of thought and conversation long after the novels have been read."[134]

27 Another Take on the Gaps

It seems extraordinary to me that no one, so far as I know, has remarked on what I consider to be the essential nature of the gaps in the reading experience to the artistic experience of silently read literary fiction. In fact, Roman Ingarden is the only author with whom I am familiar who so much as mentions the reading gap (although I do not claim an encyclopedic knowledge of the relevant literature). And what he says about it, which is really very little, suggests that, far from recognizing it as a valuable and, I think, an intended part of the literary experience of read fiction, he construes it, rather, as, for the most part, a necessary yet undesirable glitch in what should, ideally, be a continuous reading of the literary work.

Ingarden writes, in *The Cognition of the Literary Work of Art*: "For the purpose of simplicity I shall consider only the case in which a given work is read for the first time from beginning to end without interruption . . .. Of course, this is possible only with relatively short works."[135] The implication seems to be that although reading a work of fiction "from beginning to end without interruption . . . is possible only with short works," that fact does not much matter to our understanding of the read literary experience. The fact that longer works cannot be read at one go is ignored for simplicity's sake, as not being germane to the philosophy of the literary experience.

We should not, furthermore, be led astray by what Ingarden talks about later on, which might *seem* to be an acknowledgement that the reading gaps are essential, in some positive sense, to the silent reading experience of fiction. Here is what Ingarden says:

> The literary work of art can reveal itself to us in reading only in a temporally unfolding continuum of phenomena of temporal perspective, if, of

course, reading is not interrupted, which always happens when we read a novel. Thus it is not permissible to demand the kind of apprehension of a work of art which would be completed in a single "now" and encompass all its phases and strata. Such a demand would only prove that one had neither apprehended nor understood an essential feature of the literary work of art.[136]

It might seem that the contrast here is between reading a novel continuously, at one go, in which it "would be completed in a single 'now,'" a feat we cannot demand of the reader, and reading with interruptions, which is the only way novel-reading can be done. If one demanded the former, "Such a demand would only prove that one had neither apprehended nor understood an essential feature of the literary work of art." The literary work of art, on this understanding of the passage, is essentially an interrupted, "temporally unfolding continuum of phenomena of temporal perspective," not "a single 'now,'" which it could only be if, *per impossibile*, novel-reading could be temporally gapless and uninterrupted.

This, however, is a misunderstanding of the quoted passage. What are being contrasted are not interrupted and uninterrupted reading of novels, but reading of novels, whether interrupted or uninterrupted being beside the point, with the experience of visual, non-literary art works, like statues and paintings, which, although they do, of course, take time to apprehend, *are* "completed in a single 'now.'" Contrasted with statues, paintings, and the like, "the very nature of the literary work of art" is of "an ordered sequence of parts."[137] Again, the fact that the temporal experience of the literary work of art is, of necessity, gappy, with interruptions, remains, for Ingarden, an inessential accident of human nature.

There is only one section in *The Cognition of the Literary Work of Art*, so far as I am aware, where Ingarden really makes some acknowledgment of what I have been calling the gaps and afterlife of the silent reading experience. Again, the contrast here is between the experience of the read literary work and the experience of the visual arts. But Ingarden seems interested only in the "aesthetic" aspects of art works, not, as I am, in their philosophical, moral, and other "content" (at least to the extent that the two can be held distinct). Furthermore, he is not so much concerned with how we think about literary works as how we can cognize them as wholes, like paintings and statues, even though they are objects in temporal flow rather than, like paintings and statues, enduring physical objects in time. Nevertheless, he does seem to recognize the same temporal spaces that I do, in his explanation of how we can cognize read literary art works as whole entities. The literary artwork "can be reviewed . . . in acts of recollection but even then, only in condensed form or by running through its successive parts in recollection," in what I have called the afterlife. Or "we can interrupt the work after reading a part of it and assume the reflective attitude for a time in order to cognize parts of the work already read and aesthetically constituted . . .," which is to say, in what I have called the gaps. Or, finally, "we can try, during the aesthetic experience of the work, to carry out the aesthetic-reflective cognition of the individual phases of the work in new, so to speak overlaid acts of cognition."[138]

Thus, in this brief recognition of the gaps and afterlife in the read literary experience, Ingarden went some way towards acknowledgment of their role in that experience. But he failed on at least two counts. He failed to recognize just how essential interrupted reading is to the read literary experience as we know it. And he failed to realize fully what its role is, by failing to realize its importance to the expression and cognition of implied hypotheses. I have no quarrel with Ingarden's account of aesthetic cognition in the gaps and afterlife; a lot of what he says is right, if obscurely stated. What is lacking, and what I have been trying to give, is an account of the role of the gaps and afterlife in forwarding fictional literature's epistemic credentials. To that endeavor I now return.

28 Doubts

Now of course no one has ever denied that literary works can suggest, and indeed have suggested philosophical and moral theses to readers. And if those readers are talented, they may even use such theses to build philosophical and moral systems of their own. But, the doubter may insist, that does not mean that the *work* has done anything but express these naked, hence banal philosophical or moral theses that the reader-philosopher has transformed, in another work, into deep and interesting ones.

This, I think, gets to the heart of my proposal. It is perfectly true that what I have just described is not only a possible scenario, but one that has been played out many times. One is reminded, for example, of the tribute Freud paid to Dostoyevsky as an inspiration to his own work. Yet it would be nonsense to suggest that Freud's lifetime of thinking about the unconscious and the rest was just one long literary experience of the novels of Dostoyevsky.

But I am urging here that we not confuse two related, yet entirely distinct phenomena: the case in which a novel provides inspiration for a philosophy, or other system of thought, as in the case of Dostoyevsky and Freud, and the case in which the educated, general reader, of the kind

I have described previously, as a legitimate and necessary part of the literary experience, is stimulated, in the gaps and afterlife of reading a serious novel, to thinking and reasoning about the moral or philosophical or psychological hypotheses expressed therein. The former clearly is *not* an instance, at least in its entirety, of literary appreciation, although it may very well begin as such, as I presume it did with Freud's encounter with Dostoyevsky. The latter, I insist, *is* just that; and I find the notion of literary appreciation without it, where the work is such as to invite this kind of philosophical or moral thinking, as artistically impoverished as the listening to a Beethoven symphony in bits and pieces would be. Just as continuity and self-containedness are the hallmarks of the appreciation of serious classical music, in the modern tradition, philosophical and moral contemplation in the gaps and afterlife are the hallmarks of literary appreciation, where the work demands that. That, at least, is my claim.

If I am right, then the defender of the proposition theory of literary plausibility has this reply to the charge of banality. Where the banality is alleged to result from the lack of argument and analysis in the literary work, as it would in many novels, the reply is that argument and analysis occur in the gaps and afterlife, *in the reader's mind*, as part and parcel of a legitimate literary experience.

But if, it might be objected, the expression of live, deeply significant moral and philosophical hypotheses is a good-making feature of fictional literary works, it surely can't impart very *much* value. For it seems that trivial and even downright bad literary works – maudlin tear-jerkers, pulp fiction, cheap romances, low-grade science fiction – can express important moral and philosophical hypotheses that are living ones for readers of these time-wasters. Yet these works hardly seem much better for it than others of the same kind that express no such hypotheses. Doesn't this suggest that whatever there may be to the propositional theory of literary plausibility, there can't be very much to the plausibility theory of literary value, hence, not very much aesthetic significance to the propositional theory of literary plausibility, even if true?

The response must be that it is the *way* hypotheses are expressed in fictional literary works that determines whether the expression imparts great value, or little to them. For what lifts them from the banal to the interesting and significant is what happens to them in the gaps and afterlife. And what happens to them there is a function of the reader's obsession with them, which leads to, indeed compels analysis, argument, and evaluation. But what leads to the obsession? What encourages and sustains thought about the implied hypotheses, in the gaps and afterlife, or, for that matter, thought about the various other aspects of a serious literary work that it demands and encourages – thoughts about plot, character, language, and the rest?

The answer is both easy and at the same time difficult to give. It is easy to give because we all know the *general* answer. The great, the serious works of literary fiction are thick with artistic and aesthetic artifice. Their linguistic fabric is eloquent, complex (or ingeniously simple), intriguing. Plot and character are convoluted and deep. When moral or philosophical hypotheses are conveyed by such artistically and aesthetically rich materials, they become imprinted upon the reader's consciousness with an indelible brand. We find ourselves compelled, as it were, to think and reason about what we have read. That is the easy answer.

The difficult answer is to spell out in detail what specific aesthetic and artistic artifaces perform what specific functions, and how, in the process by which the reader is led, or perhaps more strongly, even *compelled* by the great author, to think and reason, in the gaps and afterlife, about the moral or philosophical hypotheses expressed in the fictional work of art. That, however, is work for another occasion; so I must really leave it here as an unpaid debt. But I think I owe at least one example, by way of a down payment.

One of the most frequent forms of praise given a work of literary fiction is that its characters have complexity and depth. "The characters are alive, multidimensional; I really cared about them," reads an advertising blurb on the back cover of a popular fictional work.[139]

Let me suggest that when we receive live and deeply significant moral or philosophical hypotheses from the discourse of fictional characters who are "alive" and "multidimensional," characters we really care about, we are encouraged, even compelled to take these hypotheses seriously, the way we tend to take to heart the opinions of friends and family whom we respect or hold in high regard. They lodge in our minds, and, and, inevitably, we think about them. Perhaps we say to ourselves, "If an admirable and deep person like that, whom I really care about, holds this opinion, then perhaps it is an opinion worth considering seriously." But if the character is one-dimensional pasteboard, why should I be persuaded to take him or her seriously? Surely that is *part* of the reason *Crime and Punishment* compels me to take the question of crime and punishment seriously, and *The Maltese Falcon* does not, as entertaining a confection as it may be.

Much more needs to be said in this regard. But I must press on. Before I do, though, a minor matter of terminology must be cleared up, which might cause trouble later.

29 Semantic Quibbles

I have referred to Ion's comments on Homer as part of his "performance," the thinking that goes on during the gaps and afterlife of silent reading as part of the "literary experience," and I suggest that the latter and the former are really two ways of doing the same thing, one suited to experiencing literature aurally, the other suited to experiencing it in the manner of a silent reader. I now want to straighten out this apparent inconsistency in terminology before going on to other matters.

First of all, I do not want to get embroiled in an argument over whether Ion's comments on Homer are part of his "performance," properly so called, or interpolations that are not literally part of the performance of Homer *qua* performance. I think it is purely a matter of semantics and do not care which way you talk. What I do want to say is that *both* the recitation of Homer, *and* the comments on Homer are part of the "literary experience," properly so called, that the Greeks had when they heard Homer recited and commented upon by Ion and his ilk.

Similarly, I do not want to get into another argument, which I also consider a purely semantic one, as to whether the thinking that goes on in the gaps and afterlife of silent novel-reading is part of what I have been calling "the performance of reading," or is an interpolation. Calling it part of the "literary experience" circumvents that question and suits my purposes. Call it part of the performance or an interpolation, I do not much care which, just as long as you consider it part of the "literary experience." That I would insist on.

And now on to other matters.

30 Unuttered Conversation

In the previous six sections I argued that an essential aspect of the serious literary experience, where the silent reading of a novel is concerned, may often, although not by any means always, include periods of thought on the part of the reader about the philosophical, moral, and other such propositions that the work may imply or overtly express, as part of its artistic purpose. These episodes of thought occur in what I called the gaps and afterlife of the work. Furthermore, it is the main thesis of this monograph that silent reading is a kind of performance: a performance in the head of a story telling. Are these two theses compatible? Can we live with them both?

The answer is "Yes." Just as the Greeks lived with an Ion who both performed a story and performed a commentary on it, *we* can live with a performance in the head that is both the performance of a story telling and a performance of a commentary on that story – when, that is to say, such a commentary is appropriate to the story. And as we have so often before done in this monograph, we can turn again to the spirit of Plato for our image.

Plato famously said in the *Sophist* (and it has served as my epigraph) that "thought and speech [are] the same, with this exception, that what is called thought is the unuttered conversation of the soul with herself."[140] Now I am no philosopher of mind, with a "theory" of consciousness. But I do think I am "in touch" with my own consciousness. And it is my experience, based on that access, which some say is privileged, that Plato has captured in this well-known characterization how, at least it *sometimes* is with me. Sometimes – indeed frequently – when I think about philosophy, or some other "serious" matter, it is in the form of an argument or conversation in the head with someone specific, like a friend with whom I have discussed the subject before or, as Plato says, sometimes it is an argument or conversation in the head with myself.

But you don't just have to take my word for it, albeit perhaps my privileged word. Frequently, my wife asks me, "Who are you talking to?," even though I am sitting across from her, just the two of us, in complete silence. The way she knows I am having a conversation in the head, she has told me, is that I make small motions with my hands and head, of which I am unaware, of just the same kind that I make, more overtly, when I am conversing aloud. And I know she is right because she has never once asked me that question, "Who are you talking to?," when I haven't been, just at that time, doing just that: having an argument or conversation in the head and been very conscious of it.

Now I am far from claiming that this is always the way everybody thinks, or that everybody thinks this way any of the time. But I am very conscious of thinking this way some significant part of the time, and particularly when I am thinking about philosophical, or other "serious" things. Plato apparently had the same impression of his own thinking; so that makes two of us. As well, my idea here, and my experience also, are perfectly captured by another "inner conversationalist," Susan Haack, who writes, about the early stage of discovery, whether scientific, philosophical, or whatever, that it "is well construed as involving a kind of inner dialogue. An inquirer tries out a conjecture; imagines possible objections and devises possible replies; figures out consequences and puts himself in the position of a possible objector, . . . and so on."[141] And if my wife is to be credited, I show behavioral evidence that this is the way I sometimes think. Furthermore, I know full well that when she spies me conversing with myself, by noticing my hand and head movements, it is almost always about those "serious," philosophical things that seem to me to most particularly characterize my "unuttered conversation." And my experience in this regard is, I believe, merely a special case of what a recent author has aptly described as "the *Joycean machine* – the stream of inner verbalization that occupies so much of our waking lives . . .."[142]

Daniel Dennett, in fact, makes the daring proposal that *thinking* might very well have had its evolutionary origin in *talking to yourself*, in particular, asking yourself questions *aloud*: "the practice of asking oneself questions [aloud] could arise as a natural side effect of asking questions of others . . .,"[143] he conjectures. The next step in this (highly speculative) story would be "*sotto voce* talking to oneself, . . . leading later to entirely silent talking to oneself,"[144] in other words, a form of conscious thought through silent speech. And if this story is somewhere in the vicinity of the truth, it then seems reasonable enough that one important vestige of the origin of consciousness is Plato's "unuttered conversation." As Dennett, another sharer in my experience of silent conversation "in the head" puts it, "Not only do we talk to ourselves silently, but sometimes we do this in a particular 'tone of voice.'"[145]

But serious, sometimes philosophical thoughts are exactly what, I have argued, we think in the gaps and afterlife of deep and aesthetically distinguished novels. So what I want to say now is that these thoughts in the gaps and afterlife are, at least for me, and, I am surmising, for many other people, experienced as something like Plato's unuttered conversation. In reading novels, in other words, I am hearing the "Ion of the mind" performing, in the gaps and afterlife, his "other" function: that of commentator on the tales he tells.

However, if Ion the commentator is part of my silent reading experience, and if, as I am suggesting, he is experienced as part of an inner conversation, why not think just the same way about Ion the story teller as well? What I hear within is a tale told by my inner rhapsode who, in the gaps and afterlife, delivers his commentary in his "other" voice, just as Ion of old. And why not say as well that sometimes I converse with my inner Ion, when he comments on the moral or philosophical content of the novels he performs to my inner ear?

My total performance in the silent reading of a novel, then, is an inner analogue to Ion's total performance, as described by Plato in the dialogue of the same name. I enact a teller of tales who also comments on their content and with whom I carry on a debate, if the circumstances warrant it. (Perhaps the Athenian citizenry debated with the historical Ion as well.

After all, Socrates did in Plato's dialogue.) The "debate" is *my* thinking about the subject matter; for my thinking, in such situations is, as Plato described it in the *Sophist*.

So what are you saying?, the skeptic will ask. Are you saying that readers of novels "hear voices"? Only the insane hear voices. Are you saying that novel-reading is a form of insanity, as Plato claimed Ion's rhapsodizing was? If you are, then you must be mad yourself, for it is an utterly mad thing to say. "Son of Sam," as the notorious serial killer of recent memory was known, "heard voices." Surely you aren't saying that novel readers are like *that*. For each will rightfully reply, as Ion to Socrates: "I doubt whether you will ever have eloquence enough to convince me that I am mad and possessed . . .."[146]

Well, good skeptic, I make no such outlandish claim. "Hearing in the head," whether it is music or speech, does not mean hallucinating. When Brahms read his score of *Don Giovanni*, he heard voices in his head, but he did not think that he was "hearing things." He was not a musical "Son of Sam." And I know no reason to believe that hearing speaking voices in the head need be hallucinating when hearing singing voices in the head is not. A person who thinks he is hearing *Don Giovanni* when he is merely hearing it in his head is hallucinating. A person reading a score of *Don Giovanni*, who knows exactly what he is doing, is hearing voices (and instruments) in the head in a perfectly benign and unproblematic sense. He is not a pathological case.

Pari passu, a person who thinks she is hearing a story being told out loud, when she is merely reading it and hearing it in the head, is a person with a problem. But when I argue, in my head, with an imagined friend, about a philosophical problem, and know exactly what I am doing, then I am hearing voices in my head in a perfectly benign and unproblematic sense. I am, in a word, *thinking*. The well-known cliché, "It's so noisy in here I can't hear myself think," taps, I believe, into a common human experience. Plato had it. I have it. Others have it too, as some of the above quotations make clear. Whether everyone who thinks has it I have no way of knowing.

31 And for Those without Voices

Once, however, one gets past the fear that "hearing voices in the head" implies hallucinating, another, perhaps more systematic, "metaphysical" fear may take its place. It is born of the reluctance of some philosophers of recent memory to countenance talk about imagistic thinking, or even, in extreme instances, the ordinary person's idea of what it means to think, or to be conscious at all.

No one, surely, is more famous, or perhaps, infamous for skepticism about the "inner life" of consciousness than Gilbert Ryle. And yet this same Gilbert Ryle wrote, in *The Concept of Mind*: "*Silent Argumentation* has the practical advantages of being relatively speedy, socially undisturbing and secret . . . ." He added: "special schooling is required to inculcate the trick of reasoning in *silent soliloquy*."[147] And although Ryle remained cautious about the pervasiveness of silent speech in thought to the last, he also, to the last, maintained its existence. "If you like – as I do not – to say that *game playing* is a 'family likeness concept,' then you ought to say – as I shall not – that *thinking* is also a 'family likeness concept' and that saying things to oneself does belong to some, but not to all members of the family."[148]

Now I am not interested in the question of whether "silent argumentation" or "silent soliloquy" requires, as Ryle thought, "special schooling," or is simply "doin' what comes naturally." What does interest me is that someone as behavioristically oriented as Ryle, and as fearful of the "ghost" of consciousness, has a place in his conceptual scheme and personal experience for both. And I ask no more of my reader than that he or she does as well. However you wish to understand "consciousness," even as in the manner of the extreme logical behaviorist, if you have a place in your conceptual scheme and experience for Ryle's "silent argumentation" or "silent soliloquy," you have the materials for a "silent storyteller" too, assuming, of course, that, as I do, you experience silently read fictional literature as a story being related to you (never mind by *whom*).

Ryle, whom I take to be the paradigm, in modern times, of "consciousness skepticism," was quite willing to make the distinction between "thinking out loud" and "thinking to yourself." Experiencing a story silently, in other words, silently reading it to yourself is, I am claiming, a species of thinking to yourself: a species of "silent soliloquy." I think the best way of describing what goes on when you read to yourself, silently, a fictional narrative, is that you are being told a story silently. If you can go that far with me, and you can also accept the notion of "silent soliloquy," as Ryle does, then it appears to me you have pretty much accepted the notion I have been pushing of silent reading of fiction as the experience of a voice "in your head" telling you a story.

There are those who will not be able to go this far with me: who will claim that they do not experience silent soliloquy, do not hear voices in their heads, even in the pristine Rylean sense. To those I can have nothing further to say. They must experience the silent reading of fiction in a way very different from my way. But what of that? Why should I think that the experience of fiction is completely uniform among us? As Kant famously said, nothing straight was ever made of human timber. I am giving an account of *my* experience of silently read fiction. I do not think that I am so unique, such a *rara avis* that others do not share my experience. For those who do not, I hope they will give an account of their experience, so we can compare notes. *Vive la différence*!

But we have yet to face an objection that was entered earlier on, and postponed until the appropriate place. The appropriate place is here, and the objection is this. If reading novels is hearing story telling in the head, as reading scores is hearing music in the head, then surely, it will be argued, just as it is agreed on all hands that someone born deaf could not read a musical score with musical understanding and appreciation, he could not read a novel with literary understanding and appreciation, which is absurd. As Richard Shusterman puts the point: "But such people do read, enjoy and understand literary works of art. Certainly their appreciation lacks an important element in the case of works built heavily on oral effects, but so does that of the congenitally blind in the case of works full of rich visual images."[149]

It is, needless to say, next to impossible for a sighted person with unimpaired hearing to imagine what the conscious life is of a person deprived of sight or hearing from birth. With that caveat on the table, I will now, as circumspectly as possible, try to deal with Shusterman's argument.

Consider the following passage from a well-known novel:

> Jones flung himself at his benefactor's feet, and taking eagerly hold of his hand, assured him his goodness to him, both now and all other times, had so infinitely exceeded not only his merit but his hopes, that no words could express his sense of it. "And I assure you, sir," said he, "your present generosity hath left me no other concern than for the present melancholy occasion."[150]

Now consider how this passage would be experienced by a reader with unimpaired hearing. The reader would clearly distinguish between the narrative voice of the novel and the voice of the character directly quoted. If read aloud, the declaimer would surely distinguish between the two voices, and read the speech of Tom Jones in what she considered the manner and tone of his voice might be, which would be a different manner and tone from that of the narrative voice. And I assume that the silent reader, whatever his or her reading skills, would experience Tom's speech in a "phenomenologically" distinct way: as speech of a character, speaking "in character." *I* think that the best way of describing how the silent reader experiences the speech is as of a character speaking "in his head," just as, if he were an accomplished score reader, he would "hear in his head" the clarinet solo in a symphony. I am also, of course, claiming that he hears the narrative voice, the voice telling him the story, that way.

What about a person born deaf? How does *she* experience Tom Jones' speech? Obviously she has no idea how the human speaking voice sounds. She has never heard one. She can perceive *that* Tom Jones is speaking directly. She knows the written signs that mark out characters' speaking from the narrative text. But she cannot experience Tom's speech "phenomenologically" in the manner of a person with unimpaired hearing, as described above, any more than she can "hear in her head" the clarinet solo in a symphony. She is, in this respect, not able to *fully* "enjoy and understand literary works of art," which is no more than Shusterman is willing to admit when he says that the "appreciation [of the deaf] lacks an important element in the case of works built heavily on oral effects . . .," works with extensive directly quoted speech being a case in point.

Thus it is clear that if the phenomenological experience we get when silently reading direct quotation in novels is anything like hearing declamation "in the head," then readers born deaf cannot have that experience, and are deficient in that respect. But that conclusion prepares us for a further one that the silent reader born deaf cannot hear "in his head" the voice of the character in *Moby Dick* when he reads the famous opening sentence "Call me Ishmael . . . ." He can indeed perceive *that* he is being (fictionally) addressed by a character in the novel who is going to tell him the story of the white whale; he cannot, however, hear it as a fictional voice "in the mind's ear," any more than he can the words of Tom Jones, or those of the teller of his story when he warns us: "Reader, I think proper, before we proceed any further, to acquaint thee that I intend to digress, through this whole history . . . ."[151]

The reader may be surprised, at this point, by the direction the argument is taking, because it is, indeed, leading inexorably to the conclusion that just as the person born deaf cannot "hear in the head" Tom Jones or Ishmael, she cannot, either, hear the "inner Ion" that I "hear" when he begins to tell me the story of "the best of times and the worst of times." The account of silent novel-reading that I am giving here will not work for the congenitally deaf. I accept this conclusion; but I do not think it is destructive of my project. Here is why.

I have carefully proceeded from what I think is the uncontroversial claim that the congenitally deaf person's reading experience is not full in regard to directly quoted speech. The option of "hearing in the head" such speech is closed to her. I see no reason not to conclude as well that in the case of the "inner Ion," her experience of silently read fiction is not full, at least in this restricted sense: she cannot experience literature *in that way*. One possible literary experience is closed to her.

Of course I never started out to give an account of the literary experience of the congenitally deaf. Such a task would require having an expertise with regard to the hearing impaired that I do not claim to have. That the congenitally deaf *do* have a rich and deep appreciation of novels and other silently read literary fiction, Shusterman rather confidently asserts, and I have, *for the sake of argument*, assumed to be the case. However, it is now the time to burst this *a priori* philosophical bubble. As a matter of empirical fact, congenitally deaf children have extreme difficulty in learning to read, and consistently perform below the base level of normal children in school – a condition which, alas, persists after they have left school, and into adulthood.[152] Thus reading competence in the congenitally deaf cannot just be confidently assumed; and how rich and deep, therefore, their experience of the novel is, compared to those with unimpaired hearing, I have no way of knowing: there is good reason for skepticism in that regard.

Until, then, we have an answer to the question of whether any of the congenitally deaf have a rich and deep appreciation of silently read fictional literature, or are severely compromised in this regard, we cannot really know whether their experience of silently read fiction is a counterexample to my account. I strongly suspect that it is not.

In any case, if the congenitally deaf for the most part *do* have a rich and deep appreciation of silently read literary fiction, then it follows that hearing a narrative "Ion in the head" is not a *necessary* condition for a rich and deep appreciation of silently read fiction, and I will leave it at that. It is for others, who are experts in the problems of the hearing impaired, to work out what the experience of literature is for them.

We can, then, put aside the notion, if we ever really seriously entertained it, that hearing voices in the head, when that is a description of thinking, as in the *Sophist*, or a description of silently reading a novel, as I suggest, implies hallucination or any other kind of psychological pathology. And we can put aside too the fear that concepts like silent voices in the head, in other words, as Ryle puts it, "silent soliloquy" must imply overly rich, imagistic models of human consciousness and thought, or that the congenitally deaf pose a counterexample to my thesis. Assuming these fears to be unfounded, I think that an illuminating way of characterizing the silent novel-reading experience is as a performance in the head of a rhapsode who, like Ion, not only tells a story but comments on its philosophical, moral, or other content, if it has any. Silently read literary fiction, in this sense, is, like music, a performing art. Its closest analogy is to the silently read musical score, where what is read we hear in the head as a musical performance of the work scored. The proposal preserves, in spirit but not in letter, the first account of silently read fiction, the Addisonian, which likens reading silently to seeing a dramatic production, in the head. But I have moved from the sense modality of sight to that of hearing.

The reader, of course, will recall that I emphatically rejected the Addisonian characterization of silently read fiction. Indeed, the theory, as I pointed out, had already received, in its own time, a devastating critique in Edmund Burke's much admired and widely read *Enquiry into the Sublime and Beautiful*. The indictment read that it was not within the power of language, or in its nature, to arouse visual imagery to the extent required by theory, nor was it within the power of the human imagination to entertain such elaborate visual imagery in the first place. The theory was doubly damned.

But it might now be plausibly asked why, if the Burkean critique is good against the Addisonian theory of silently read fiction, it should not be good against my neo-Addisonian theory as well? Why, in other words, should it be any more plausible to think of the experience of silently read fiction as an experience of aural mental imagery than of visual mental imagery? Why do ears have it over eyes in this regard? This is a weighty objection, and it requires close attention before I close.

32 Sight and Sound

There are places where philosophy can't go: places where it can't help very much. And this may be one of them. For the question before us is why it should seem more plausible to characterize an event as sound in the head rather than sight in the head, hearing in the head rather than seeing in the head. But the place of these sense modalities, hearing and seeing, in the human animal's perceptual system is so hemmed in by scientific considerations that only fools would rush in where empirical science has so much with which to occupy itself. The function of eye and ear in human biology is a subject for evolutionary theory, brain science, neuro-physiology, cognitive science, and the psychology of perception. It is not for the philosopher of art to make *a priori* pronouncements from his armchair about this very difficult subject. What follows, then, is offered as the merest of suggestions, from the point of view of what I *hope* is *common sense*.

What must be understood straightaway is that I am certainly not denying to human beings the ability to entertain mental images: to "see" in the head. What is being maintained, rather, is that silent novel-reading as an experience of continuous visual imagery in the head, as if one were seeing in the mind's eye, in the manner of a cinematic or theatrical production, is beyond what the human imagination can accomplish. That seeing in the head may be a *part* of some people's novel-reading need not be denied. What is being denied is that it can possibly carry the full burden of the narrative experience, or, for that matter, a very large share of the burden. The mind cannot do it; language cannot facilitate it; language is not meant to facilitate it.

Why, then, should I think it more plausible to characterize the experience of silent novel-reading as a through and through hearing in the head: a continuous hearing in the head of an Ion-like storyteller? Why should the human mind be able to perform such an extended exercise in mental hearing but not mental seeing?

There are really two questions here: Why do I think human beings *can* perform as described *vis-à-vis* sound? And what do I think the reason is that they *cannot vis-à-vis* sight? I don't claim to have anything conclusive to say in response to either question. The best I can offer is some circumstantial evidence.

In the first place, it has been one of the theses of this book that the silent reading of a novel has a direct analogy to the silent reading of a musical score. We *know* from the reliable testimony of those who are able to read scores at the optimal level, and from well-established historical facts, that they hear in their heads full performances of extended musical works. So we have adequate empirical evidence that the human mind has the ability to hear in the head far beyond the ability to see in the head. And although being able to read musical scores at the level necessary to hear full musical performances of extended works in the head is a rare human ability, the ubiquitousness among the human species of language, both spoken and read, provides an obvious reason for believing that reading a narrative text, and hearing it fully in the head, as a spoken narrative, is not a rare human ability but, unlike its musical analogue, a common one.

In the second place, it might be appropriate at this point in what is, to be sure, a highly speculative argument, based on somewhat anecdotal evidence, to introduce a suggestive bit of "expert" empirical data, cited by Gregory Currie and Ian Ravenscroft, in their intriguing book, *Recreative Minds.* They write: "It is estimated that 50 per cent of people with schizophrenia suffer auditory hallucinations, which involve the experience of someone speaking to or about the subject, while 15 per cent have visual hallucinations and 5 per cent tactile hallucinations."[153] What might the significance of this data be to the present proceedings?

Currie and Ravenscroft hypothesize that "delusions and hallucinations in schizophrenia are due to a failure to identify imaginings . . .."[154] Which is to say, the schizophrenic, when he is in the grips of an auditory, a visual, or a tactile hallucination mistakenly believes that his auditory, or visual, or tactile imagining is not an imagining at all but a perception. We can tell the difference between our perceptions and our imaginings; he, frequently, cannot, and typically mistakes the latter for the former.

Now why should auditory delusions and hallucinations be so much more common than visual or tactile ones? The answer that immediately springs to mind, given my hypothesis that our capacity for realizing sounds "in the head" seems to far outstrip our capacities *vis-à-vis* any of the other sense modalities, is that just because auditory hearings in the head are so much more vivid and complete in the unafflicted person, and more easily accomplished, they are more easily, and more frequently, therefore, taken for perceptions by those suffering from schizophrenia. (And note well that it is "speaking voices" that are what the schizophrenic "hears.") The facts seem to fit the theory.

Of course I fully realize that I am in very deep waters here. The study of mental disease is for experts, not amateurs with a philosophical axe to grind. I offer this data, then, as, at best, corroborating evidence, but at worst, after all, not obviously disconfirming.

In the third place, to return to the anecdotal, there is ample testimony to the effect that many human beings, from Plato to the present, have believed that they have experienced their own thinking, at least at times, as, in Plato's words, "the unuttered conversation of the soul with herself." In other words, many people report that, at least at times, they experience thinking as the hearing of a voice in the head. The experience seems neither pathological nor in any other way bizarre. And the intimate connection that so many have drawn, between language and thought, even to the extent of conflating the two, is too obvious a point to belabor.

One can add to this the observation that the pace of reading seems to match more or less the pace of at least ordinary thinking, whereas the pace of visual imagining in the mind does not (which was one of Burke's more telling points). If this is true, it seems far more plausible to conceive of novel-reading as hearing rather than seeing in the head.

But that being the case, it should not seem difficult to accept that the act of silent reading produces a hearing in the head of those same words spoken and, in the case of silently read narrative fiction, the spoken words of the story teller. This is how I think I experience the silent reading of a story; and I doubt that I am some kind of weirdo in this regard. It is, of course, always dangerous to trust one's own introspection as if it were transparent and incorrigible. However, it must count for something, nor, clearly, am I alone in this at least seeming experience of thinking as speaking in the head; and it appears to be an easy step from that to the experience of silent fiction-reading as speaking in the head, in the form of the story teller's voice, although I have no one's word to take for it other than my own. And so I will have to leave it at that.

But now to our second, and I think much deeper question. If I am right about the comparative capacities of human beings to see and hear in the head, the capacity for the latter being far greater than for the former, what explanation might be adduced for the disparity? I say, straightaway, that I do not have an explanation. Nonetheless, I think there is a marked difference in the ways we experience sights and sounds – a difference in their "phenomenology," if you will – that might perhaps lie at the heart of the differences in our capacities to image sights and sounds, respectively, in the head. It is a difference worth at least a cursory glance.

Ordinary language seems to have it that we see *things* but hear *sounds*. Thus, I say that I hear an oboe, or that I hear the sound of an oboe. I say likewise that I see a tree; but I never say that I see the sight of a tree. And when I see a tree, the intentional object of my seeing is the tree, whereas, when I hear the oboe the intentional object of my hearing is the sound of the oboe, not the oboe.

Furthermore, whatever conscious state of perceiving I am put in by seeing the tree and its causal connection with my perceiving it informs me how it is with the tree: the tree is discovered to me. But it seems as if the sounds of the oboe do no such thing for me either with regard to the oboe, or to the vibrations of the air that are the immediate cause of my hearing the sounds. Thomas Reid, one of the most acute philosophers of perception in the modern philosophical tradition, long ago pointed out the interesting fact that with regard to some of the qualities we perceive, *some* (but not *all*) of the so-called secondary qualities, we have no trouble concentrating our attention on the *sensations*, rather than on the objective qualities that are their cause. Whereas with others, principally the qualities of *sight*, we cannot do that (or at least we do it, if at all, with great difficulty). Thus, as Reid puts the point, "the sensations belonging to secondary qualities are an object of our attention, while those belonging to the primary qualities are not."[155]

And, therefore, a recent commentator on Reid explains, "we are able much more easily to form," on Reid's view, "a distinct notion of the sensations involved in our perception of the secondary qualities than we are of the sensations associated with the primary qualities . . .."[156]

Sounds are clear examples of qualities that we perceive as sensations.

They have no being, for us, as perceivers, apparently, *except* as sensations: as subjective states, even though we assume that there are qualities external to us that cause them, and that we *also* call "sounds."

It appears, then, that sounds are experienced by us as purely subjective phenomena. What we hear are sounds. We see trees, we do not see tree experiences; but we hear sound experiences and nothing more. Sounds are, so to say, a purely mental experience. Does this have something to do with why our capacity for hearing in the head exceeds our capacity for seeing in the head? I suspect that it does though I am at a loss to explain what the connection is. I will have to leave it at that; leave it, that is, with the acknowledgment of my own ignorance in the matter.

33 Parsimony

I began the argument of this monograph with some remarks on the ontology of art. I said, it will be recalled, that common sense tells us music, at least in the modern classical tradition, is a performing art, and the novel is not. And I expressed the view that although common sense is right if it keeps its distance, closer philosophical scrutiny might well induce us to revise common sense considerably. That revision you now have before you.

I have argued that the silent reading of fictional literature, the novel in particular, can be understood as something very like a performance. And I tried to show how this kind of performance might be connected to, and emerge from the experience of fictional literature in an institutional setting that dates from antiquity, and precedes the era of silent reading.

But when I say that the silent reading of fictional literature *can* be understand as a kind of performance, it seems to suggest some room for choice. Understand it that way if you like, another way if you prefer – that sort of thing. And I do suppose that is what I meant to suggest. At least I do not wish to present my conclusion as if I thought it was the result of a knock down argument.

However, if one can, yet need not necessarily construe the novel as a performing art, in the way described on these pages, why *should* one construe it that way? One reason might be that it seems to you to capture the way you think you experience novels when you read them. That certainly is one, and, for me the major reason why I am inclined to construe them that way. Here is another reason, of a familiar type.

I began, to repeat, by saying that according to common sense silently read literature, in particular, the novel, is not a performing art. In this it is in the same boat as traditional painting and sculpture, so-called auto-graphic arts. Unlike painting and sculpture, however, the novel is not an autographic art: it is an allographic one. That is to say, there are tokens of the type.

On the other hand, what the tokens are – *not*, remember, printed copies of the novel but "readings" of the novel – seemed to us at the outset to be very different kinds of entities from performances of symphonies. Worse still, they seemed to us to be very different kinds of entities from dra-matic performances, even though novels and plays are all works of literary fiction, and the latter can be silently read. Fictional literature, in this respect, we said was a mixed bag: so, at least, common sense would have it.[157]

But the law of parsimony, sometimes known as Ockham's razor, tells us that assuming only as many principles as necessary is the rational policy to pursue. And in the present instance, that policy directs us to construe silent readings of fictional works such as novels as performances. For in so doing we reduce the kinds of tokens in fictional literature from two to one: from "readings" and "performances" to "performances" alone, the former being a variety of the latter, as are silent readings of musical scores. Monism is preferable to dualism if it works. It seems to work here.

34 More Parsimony?

I suggested, in the previous section, that considerations of parsimony en-courage us to construe silently read fictional literature, and, in particular, the novel, as a performing art. If one accepts Nelson Goodman's distinc-tion between autographic and allographic arts, then, on that view, one accepts that painting and sculpture, for instance, are autographic arts, and music, in the modern Western classical tradition, an allographic art. Liter-ature, like music, is an allographic art; but, unlike music, silently read lit-erature (as opposed to drama and recited poetry) does not seem to be a performing art. Thus there are, *prima facie*, two kinds of allographic arts: the performed and the non-performed ones. The principle of parsimony, or Ockham's razor admonishes us to, if possible, construe silently read fiction, like music, drama and recited poetry, a performing art; and I have tried so to construe it in the preceding pages.

But why stop here? Why not push the principle of parsimony further still, so as to break down the Goodmanian distinction, assumed from the outset, between autographic and allographic arts: between, that is, arts without and arts with multiple instances? Painting and sculpture are the paradigms of autographic art. If these could be reclassified as allographic arts, then we would have gone a long way towards fully satisfying the law of parsimony, and making out a case for there being no autographic/allographic distinction at all: *all* of the arts would then be arts with multiple instances.

It should be pointed out straightaway that not all of the visual or graphic arts are even *prima facie* autographic. Clearly prints and multiple statues cast from the same mold are not. Each individual print, for example, that is pulled from a wood block, is an instance of the work: clearly there is a distinction here between work and instance. And it is this kind of visual art that, I imagine, emboldened the late Frank Sibley, among others, to argue that, appearances to the contrary notwithstanding, painting and sculpture may, at least in principle if not in practice, have instances as well.

Sibley's proposal is that such paradigm cases of autographic art as the *Mona Lisa*, for example, may not be unique physical objects at all but what he calls "abstract entities." This is to say that they can be instantiated in more than one place by reproducing at that place their "visual appearance." There is no need to identify the *Mona Lisa* as that painted object hanging in the Louvre. "On the hypothesis that other manifestations of the appearance of the *Mona Lisa* are possible and that the work itself is abstract, it is irrelevant what the physical nature of other bearers is and how the appearance is produced, by colour photography, printing, transparency, or whatever, so long as it is produced."[158]

Nor does it bother Sibley that, at present, there are no possible ways of fully realizing, by other physical means, the visual appearance that a painting or other so-called autographic visual art work presents to the viewer. "Doubts about the practical possibility of reinstantiating a type carry no weight in the argument whether the *Mona Lisa* is or is not a type [i.e. abstract entity]. At most they would show that if it is an abstract entity, there may in fact never be more than one instantiation."[159]

I will not go any further into Sibley's attempt to make his suggestion plausible. Rather, what I want to do is examine it from the point of view of parsimony, and in light of my claim that silent novel-reading, and the like, be construed as performing arts. What must be noticed, straightaway, is that the parsimony Sibley's suggestion would achieve, if workable, is to obliterate the distinction between autographic and allographic arts: if it works, there are *only* allographic arts. But the distinction between performing arts, and non-performing arts would remain. *Absolute* parsimony would not be achieved. That would require a separate argument.

We have, after all, the art of the print, which is counted on all hands to be an allographic art. But when the print maker pulls a print from, say, a wood block, that surely is not a performance, as the pianist's "pulling" of a performance from the score of Beethoven's *Hammerklavier* Sonata surely *is*. Prints are not, in any obvious way, performances, or print-pullers performers. A musical performer is an artist in her own right; and musical performances differ in aesthetically and artistically relevant ways. However, pulling prints is a purely mechanical or craftsman-like proce-dure that results either in a satisfactory print or an unsatisfactory one, depending upon whether or not the thing has been done competently. There is no point in comparing a print pulled by Smith with one pulled by Jones, from the same block, if they are both "correct," as one would compare, critically, Rudolf Serkin's performance of a sonata with one by Myra Hess. And if instances of the *Mona Lisa* were produced, they, like prints pullled from the block, would not be candidates for "performance," nor the people who made them "performers."

Thus, if there is an attempt to make out a case for painting or print-making as performing arts, it would seem that the performer must be the viewer himself, and his viewing experience the performance, just as, in the case of silently read fiction, the reader is the performer, the experi-ence of reading the performance. In the visual arts, as in silent reading, the performer would be performing to himself. Is this a possible or plau-sible move?

Perhaps the most obvious difference between the visual arts and the arts *traditionally* recognized as performing arts is the existence of a "notation" in the latter from which an experience of the work must be "realized." I am thinking here, of course, of the dramatic arts, and music in the modern Western classical tradition. Furthermore, in the usual circum-stances, the way one realizes the experience of such works is through their performance, with the performer or performers as the means by which the experience is made available. And even in the highly unusual case of silent score-reading at the optimal level, the score reader must realize a performance *from* the notation, as performer to himself. You can't simply "look at" a score, contemplate it visually, to realize the music. One sense modality must be "translated," as it were, into another by a complex act of comprehension, relating symbol to sound.

But it seems otherwise in the case of the visual arts, whether or not they are autographic. Unlike the arts of non-dramatic literary fiction, such as epic poem and lyric, they have no history of performance one can point to as preceding and "leading into" their non-performance stage. Indeed, it is hard to imagine what a "performance" of a painting would be. (A woman dressed up and posing as La Gioconda?) A novel can be performed, which is to say, read aloud to an audience by a dramatic narrator, as Ion recited Homer. How would one "perform" the *Mona Lisa*? And what might the painterly art form be like that was performed, and preceded the non-performance stage that the *Mona Lisa* represents? Before there was writing, before there were texts, the epic could only exist as a performing art. But before there was *what* could painting and sculpture only exist as *what*? Before it was painting and sculpture what was it? "Nothing," seems the only sensible reply.

When one thinks of the difference between the literary and musical arts, and the visual arts, be they the autographic or allographic ones, in regard to our interactions with individual works, it seems to me that the direct, "confrontational" nature of our involvement with the latter looms large. One just *is* in the presence of the *Mona Lisa*: it is a face-to-face encounter. One has to go through an elaborate procedure of "processing," either oneself, or through the activities of others, to "face the music." It is here that performance intercedes between work and audience. One is not face to face with Beethoven's Fifth Symphony when one is face to face with the score.

I do not claim that I have "proven" by these considerations that the notion of painting and sculpture as performing arts is an unintelligible one. But if the philosophical impulse to interpret them as such is powered solely by the quest for parsimony, then it appears to me to be underpowered. There is a good deal of *prima facie* plausibility to the notion of silently read fiction as a performing art. There is none, so far as I can see, for such a proposal *vis-à-vis* the visual arts. Philosophical ingenuity at a pretty high level will have to be marshaled to convince the skeptical that the visual arts as performing arts is a live option, within the usual framework in which the work-performance distinction resides. I do not say the thing is impossible. I do say that it will be a very hard sell.

But before I leave off these matters and press on to my conclusion I must turn to two even more daring and radical attempts than Sibley's to dissolve the autographic/allographic distinction, and consider whether they provide any firmer basis for the notion of painting, sculpture, and the rest as arts of performance. The first is Gregory Currie's proposal that all art works are what he calls "action types." Here is the general idea:

> Consider Beethoven's action in putting together that structure of sounds which we associate with his Fifth Symphony. We can describe that action in various ways, but one way to describe it would be to say that it consisted in Beethoven arriving at a certain sound structure at a certain time in a certain way. That event token has four constitutive objects: Beethoven, the sound structure arrived at, a particular time, and the way of arriving at that structure. But somebody else could have arrived at the same sound structure in

the same way at a different time. That possible token, and the actual token involving Beethoven are tokens of the same type. That type is the work that we call 'Beethoven's Fifth Symphony.'[160]

As should be clear, the same analysis can be worked on any kind of fine art you like: Jane Austen's arriving at a certain word structure (or whatever) at a certain time in a certain way, Leonardo's arriving at a certain painterly structure (or whatever) at a certain time in a certain way, and so on. Currie's ontology of art is a completely monistic one. It's action types all the way down.

Currie is fully aware of how strange, how counterintuitive, how remote from our ordinary "art-talk" his conception of the work of art as "action type" seems to be. And he expends a good deal of philosophical skill and logical ingenuity in trying to bridge the gap between his rather daring proposal and ordinary artistic sense and sensibility. But it is no part of *my* project to evaluate the results of his effort in this regard. What is of concern to me is whether Currie's way of banishing the autographic from the ontology of art also implies, or at least makes easier, the dissolving of the distinction between performance and non-performance arts. And in order to answer this question we need one further piece of Currie's analysis: what he calls the artist's "heuristic path," which is to say, "the artist's achievement in arriving at that pattern or structure," "the way in which the artist arrived at the final product," "in what ways the artist drew on existing works for his inspiration, and how far the product was the result of an original conception," "what problems the artist had to resolve in order to achieve his end result, and how he resolved them."[161]

The artist, then, on Currie's view, neither creates the work nor discovers it: "the artist performs it." Which is to say, "The work is the action type which he performs in discovering the structure of the work."[162] And the action type that is the work consists in the discovering of the structure of the work, *S, through the heuristic path, H.* In other words, if two artists discover the same structure through different heuristic paths, the performances are different action types, and hence, different works of art, their identical structure to the contrary notwithstanding.

But if all artists are, *qua* artists, *performers*, it would seem that the work/performance distinction has, for Currie, gone by the boards. There are no performances of works; there are only performance works, performances which are works.

That, however, is not the conclusion Currie reaches nor, I am inclined to think, any more plausible a conclusion for Currie than it would have been for Sibley. Indeed, it seems clear that Currie is quite anxious to keep something like the the ordinary concept of work performance intact. For he writes: "However, I shall use the expression 'enact' for what the artist does; to say that the artist performs the work, while true, invites confusion with what, say, the orchestra does when it produces an instance of the work. These are two very different things."[163]

Of course this still leaves open the possibility of construing all art works as "enactments," in Currie's sense, and the individual arts "performing" arts in the usual sense, paintings, statues, and the like included. There is no evidence Currie wants to go in that direction (nor, for that matter, in my direction, of construing silent readings as performances, the silent reading arts as performing arts). And whatever considerations were adduced, in the discussion of Sibley, against the notion of the visual arts as performing arts seem equally good in regard to Currie as well. There seems no more reason on Currie's view, than on Sibley's, to construe the visual arts as performing arts.

Currie's thesis, that the work of art be construed as an action type which the artist performs in discovering the structure of the work, has been heavily criticized, and, until recently, it looked as if the attempt to construe all works of art as performances was dead in the water. It would be beside the point for me to go into the critique of Currie's position any further here. But we now have, in David Davies' recent book, *Art as Performance*, a subtle and systematic attempt to revive the general claim that art works, *all* art works, are indeed performances, while eschewing the thesis that what the artist performs is an action *type*. And although it would certainly take us too far from the subject of this monograph to present a detailed account of Davies' complex and subtle theory, I do think it demands some attention, all the more so because Davies gives the conventional "performing arts" a careful look.

In its most concise form, Davies' concept of the art work can be stated as follows: "the work itself, as the unit of criticism and appreciation, is to be identified not with a specific focus, but with a performance whereby a particular focus is specified . . .."[164]

What Davies means by the "specific focus" is what we would *ordinarily* mean by the work of art, or, if it is an allographic art, the instantiation of it that ordinarily acquaints us with the work. But for Davies *it* is not the work of art; rather, the work of art is the action, the "performance" whereby that particular object, the focus of our immediate attention in our experience of the art work, was created, or, as Davies puts it, "specified."

There is no need for us to have spelled out in detail the subtleties and complexities of Davies' version of art as performance, which are considerable, or how it differs radically from Currie's version, and why. We can, therefore, cut to the chase, and see how Davies factors into the equation what we normally think of as performances, in what we normally think of as the performing arts. Davies distinguishes, as anyone must, between works and their performances. The former he calls *performed works*, the latter *work-performances*. And he then confronts the question, as anyone theorizing about performed works and work-performances must, as to what the relationship *is* between the two. As Davies surveys the scene,

> Two alternative accounts of this relationship have found favor amongst theorists. Some have held that the product of the artist's generative activity is a set of constraints upon the class of legitimate performances of the work . . ... The alternative account, most famously endorsed by Goodman, iden- tifies the work not with something that establishes a set of constraints on right performances, but, rather, with the class of performances satisfying that set of constraints.[165]

As I do, and for somewhat (but not altogether) similar reasons, Davies opts for the former alternative. The reason, in its most general form, is simply that on the Goodmanian view, the artist can seldom be said to ever have completed his work, since if the work is the class of all its perform- ances, there are usually going to be performances after the composer's death, which means that the class of performances, and, therefore, the work, remains incomplete after the composer's death, which is, to say the least, a highly implausible result. Mozart left his great C-minor Mass, alas, unfinished; but Beethoven's Ninth Symphony surely is complete (and thank God for that). As Davies puts the point:

> For the performance theorist, the work-focus is that which completes the artist's motivated manipulations of the vehicular medium. Given that those manipulations so completed are to be conceived as a "doing," usually by a single agent, the work-focus must be something that can plausibly be said to complete such a doing . . ... Thus, for the performance theorist, the work- focus in the performance arts is most plausibly viewed as including a set of constraints that is normative for the class of performances of the work, and that therefore indirectly seems to articulate an artistic statement through those performances.[166]

Now Davies, like the rest of us, must deal with all of the sticky metaphysi- cal questions attaching to the details of the relation of performance, in the "performing arts," ordinarily so-called, to the work and to its notation. And there are many of those questions to which Davies and I would give conflicting answers. Those matters need not concern us here.

But there is one very important point, of direct relevance to present concerns, on which we are in total agreement: performances, ordinarily so-called, are works of art in their own right, apart from the works they are performances of. Thus, in Davies' terminology, *work-performances* are *performance-works*. And, he avers: "The primary reason underlying the claim that work-performances are performance-works is that our critical and appreciative discourse about work-performances has those features . . . distinctive of our discourse about artworks."[167] Furthermore, he affirms, as I have done, that one can realize a performance, in the head, without the usual performance intermediaries. He writes:

> There may be individuals who are able to *imaginatively* realize the relevant qualities of at least some works in the performance arts in the absence of a *public* performance – for example, individuals who can "hear" a piece of music when reading a score. To the extent that such mental "acts" are exercises of individual capacities, we may regard them as "private performances," instantiations of the relevant properties of the work *by* the invividual in question *in foro interno*.[168]

Of course Davies, to be consistent with his overall view of art works, *tout court*, as performances, must construe performances, ordinarily so-called, as performance-[art]works *themselves*, which is to say, he must construe them not as sound products, sound "objects," but as, so to speak, second order performance art works. As Davies puts this rather (to me) bizarre point: "*Appreciating* such a performance-event, like appreciating the work of which it is a performance, is a matter of locating a *focus of appreciation* – the performance event and artistic statement it articulates – in the context of a broader performance through which that focus is specified," which would include, among other things, taking "account of manipulations of the medium prior to that [performance] event – rehearsals of a musical piece or play, and changes made in the performance-event as a result of developments and insights arising in those rehearsals."[169]

Without carrying the analysis of Davies' views any further than this, which would not serve present purposes, we need only observe that *so far*, Davies' performance theory of art, for all of its novel features, is consistent with the thesis being advanced here, that silent readings of literary fiction are to be construed as themselves silent performances. Whether Davies himself would want to accept this thesis is, of course, another question. And it is no part of my business to try to fashion his theory to suit my purposes. It suffices to say that in acknowledging the performance status of silent score-readings, Davies has taken what I have treated, in my argument, as the first crucial step in that direction. That having been said, we can now press on to the conclusion.

35 Reading as Act

The distinction between autographic and allographic arts has, we have seen, been under some skeptical scrutiny by philosophers in recent years, with ontological parsimony certainly a serious consideration. And in proposing the hypothesis of silent fiction-reading as a performing art I have myself adduced parsimony as an attractive feature of the hypothesis. But the argument from parsimony does not carry all that much weight with me; and if I were relying solely on it to tip the scales, I myself would not consider them tipped. Rather, what appeals to me about the proposal of silent fiction-reading as a performing art is its inherent plausibility: it captures, better than any way I know of, my own reading experience. And before I close I want to adduce yet another aspect of that experience, which, I believe, but cannot be certain, must be shared by others, and which appears to me to point in the direction of reading as performance.

Those, like myself, who are fortunate enough to have lived through at least some of the "radio days," in America, frequently contrast radio drama with the television variety by pointing out that listeners to radio drama had to "do more work" than television viewers. We had to "construct," in the imagination, the visual parts of the drama that radio, of course, could not provide, but that television serves up to them on a silver platter, as it were, no effort required. (Of course I am not suggesting that the radio listener produced a *complete* sequence of visual images in the head corresponding to the events of the radio drama for the same reasons Burke adduced for its not being done in the case of written narrative.)

The argument, needless to say, is a value-laden one, the supposed implication being that radio drama was a better art form because it made more demands on its audience – required listeners to be "active" participators in the artistic experience, "collaborators," as it were, whereas the television viewer is a completely passive subject, i.e. a "couch potato."[170] In the observations to follow I want to completely cleanse this argument of its purported evaluational implication. So cleansed, it makes a valid descriptive point relevant to present concerns, namely, that as an artistic medium, the radio play, in contrast not only to the television play, but to legitimate theater and narrative cinema as well, demands of the reader *a mental act* of the imagination to supply the visual material that radio cannot.

But, and this is my point, the contrast between silently read fiction and *all* performed drama and poetry is even starker than that between radio drama and visual drama, *vis-à-vis* the active work of the audience; for the audience to silently read fiction has, essentially, to "construct" the whole narrative from a non-sensual medium. The radio play leaves out the visual but provides the sonic; silent cinema leaves out the sonic but provides the visual; and the sound film and legitimate theater, of course, provide both.[171] Silently read literary fiction, however, *leaves out both*. If, therefore, you think of silent reading as an action, an activity, it is, from this point of view, a far more elaborate and laborious activity than that required for the above-named, since they at least serve up on the silver platter material for *one* of the sense modalities, television, spoken drama, and sound movies material for both sight and hearing.

To pursue the point a step further, I think it is fair to state that, for most of us, reading a novel is a more labor intensive activity than watching a drama. And this has nothing to do with the inherent difficulties of the art works in question, which is to say, the difficulties they may present for understanding, interpretation, appreciation. Thus, it is certainly less demanding on one's powers of concentration to read a shilling shocker than to read a serious novel. But I think it is a more or less universal experience that when you are too tired to read, you are not too tired to listen and watch.[172]

The point is that in one obvious sense, silently reading literary fiction, unlike listening to and watching it, is an act, an activity of the agent. Of course it might be replied to this that the appreciation of any work of art requires the mental activities of imagination, understanding and perception. But the obvious answer is that the silent reading of literary fiction requires *those* activities as well, in addition to the act, so to speak, of *bringing forth* the artistic object for those other activities. It is, in an obvious sense, an activity, an action to play a piano sonata in order to experience it, where merely listening to it played by someone else is not. In somewhat the same obvious sense, it is an act, an activity to silently read a novel in order to experience it, where listening to it (say) on a recording for the blind is not. And, of course, the comparison is chosen with purposeful intent. For the act, the activity of reading is, as the argument of this monograph has tried to show, something very like a performance.

In sum, silently reading a novel is experienced, by me at least, as an act in the above sense. And the act seems to me to be more like a performance act, in the ways described in the preceding pages, than it is like any other act that it might be thought to resemble. Once perceived as an act, one must decide what kind of an act it is. Given what kind of an object a novel is, given what kind of an experience the silent reading of one is, given the art-historical context in which the silent reading of literary fiction has evolved, performance-act seems to me the most likely candidate. And it is my experience, not parsimony, that drives me most strongly to that conclusion.

For those to whom parsimony weighs heavily in the balance, as it does not, particularly, for me, there *is* parsimony in construing the silent reading of fiction as a performing art. There is *more* parsimony, of course, in construing all of the fine arts, across the board, as performing arts. And there are those, as we have seen, who are willing to take that step, counter-intuitive though it may seem. Those who value parsimony more than I do may attempt to take it. For my own part, a little parsimony is enough.

Notes

1 Nelson Goodman, *Languages of Art: An Approach to a Theory of Symbols* (Indianapolis: Bobbs-Merrill, 1968), pp. 113–122.
2 Ibid., Chapter V.
3 In the past I have defended something like an extreme Platonist account of the work/performance distinction, as has Jerrold Katz. My views are to be found in three essays, "Platonism in Music: A Kind of Defense," "Platonism in Music: Another Kind of Defense," and "Orchestrating Platonism," all reprinted in my *The Fine Art of Repetition: Essays in the Philosophy of Music* (New York: Cambridge University Press, 1993), as well as, more recently, in my *Introduction to a Philosophy of Music* (Oxford: Clarendon Press, 2002), Chapter 11. Katz's position is stated in *Realistic Rationalism* (Cambridge, Mass.: MIT Press, 1998), pp. 166–170.
4 Moderate Platonism in music is defended by Jerrold Levinson in his two essays, "What a Musical Work Is," and "What a Musical Work Is, Again," both in his *Music, Art and Metaphysics: Essays in Philosophical Aesthetics* (Ithaca, New York: Cornell University Press, 1990).
5 I am reminded by my friend, the biblical scholar Catherine Kravitz, that there are at least fragments of the Old Testament that some conjecture to be as early as the tenth century BC. And the *Gilgamesh* is also probably earlier than the *Iliad* and *Odyssey*. Whether the *Gilgamesh* is part of our literary canon I suppose is arguable. And although most of our Bible is certainly part of our canon, it is later than the Homeric poems. In any event, these questions are not relevant to my concerns, and nothing I say really turns on them.
6 Plato, *The Dialogues of Plato*, trans. B. Jowett (New York: Random House, 1937), vol. I, p. 660.
7 Ibid., pp. 659–660.
8 Ibid., p. 660.
9 Ibid., p. 285.
10 Ibid.
11 Ibid., pp. 288–289.
12 Ibid., p. 482.

13 Aristotle, *Poetics*, trans. Richard Janko (Indianapolis: Hackett, 1987), p. 41.

14 Gilbert Ryle, *On Thinking*, ed. Konstantin Kolenda (Totowa, New Jersey: Rowman and Littlefield, 1979), p. 35.

15 Ibid.

16 Saint Augustine, *Confessions*, trans, R. S. Pine-Coffin (Baltimore: Penguin Books, 1961), p. 178. My italics.

17 Gilbert Ryle, *Plato's Progress* (Cambridge: Cambridge University Press, 1966), p. 24.

18 Paul Saenger, *Space Between Words: The Origins of Silent Reading* (Stanford: Stanford University Press, 1997), p. 8.

19 Ibid., p. 13.

20 Ibid., p. 83.

21 Ibid., p. 257.

22 Jette Barnholdt Hansen, "From Invention to Interpretation: The Prologues to the First Court Operas Where Oral and Written Culture Meet," *The Journal of Musicology*, 20 (2003), p. 563n. The opinion is attributed to Jan Lindhardt, *Tale og skrift: To kulturer* (Copenhagen: Munksgaard, 1987), p. 53. Not having Danish, I cannot verify the claim.

23 Hansen, "From Invention to Interpretation," p. 563.

24 John Locke, *An Essay concerning Human Understanding*, ed. Peter H. Nidditch (Oxford: Clarendon Press, 1975), p. 407.

25 Ibid., p. 105.

26 I take the concept of "seeing in" from Richard Wollheim. See his *Painting as an Art* (Princeton: Princeton University Press, 1987), pp. 46–75.

27 Edmund Burke, *A Philosophical Enquiry into the Origin of Our Ideas of the Sublime and Beautiful*, ed. Adam Phillips (Oxford: Oxford University Press, 1990), p. 157.

28 Alexander Gerard, *An Essay on Taste* (3rd edn; Edinburgh, 1780), p. 277.

29 Joseph Addison, "On the Pleasures of the Imagination," Paper VIII (No. 418, Monday, June 30, 1712), *The Spectator*, ed. Alexander Chalmers (New York: D. Appleton, 1879), vol. V, p. 68.

30 Thomas Reid, *Thomas Reid on Logic, Rhetoric and the Fine Arts: Papers on the Culture of the Mind*, ed. Alexander Broadie (University Park: Pennsylvania State University Press, 2004), p. 285.

31 Ibid., p. 286.

32 Alexander Baumgarten, *Reflections on Poetry*, trans. Karl Aschenbrenner and William B. Holther (Berkeley and Los Angeles: University of California Press, 1954), p. 38.

33 Ibid.

34 Ibid, p. 39.

35 Ibid.

36 Ibid., p. 42.

37 Ibid., p. 52.

38 Thomas Reid, *Essays on the Intellectual Powers of Man, The Works of Thomas*

Reid, ed. William Hamilton (8th edn; Edinburgh: James Thin, 1895), vol. I, p. 496. My italics.

39 Ludwig Wittgenstein, *Zettel*, trans. G. E. M. Anscombe, ed. G. E. M. Anscombe and G. H. von Wright (Berkeley and Los Angeles: University of California Press, 1975), p. v.

40 Ibid., p. 44^e (#243).

41 Ibid.

42 Ibid., p. 44^e (#244).

43 I am not the first to notice these passages concerning the experience of stories in the *Zettel*. See Frank Palmer, *Literature and Moral Understanding: A Philosophical Essay on Ethics, Aesthetics, Education, and Culture* (Oxford: Clarendon Press, 1992), p. 109.

44 Burke, *Philosophical Enquiry*, p. 149.

45 Ibid., p. 150.

46 Ibid., p. 149.

47 Ibid., p. 152.

48 Michael Ayers, *Locke: Epistemology and Ontology* (London and New York: Routledge, 1991), vol. I, p. 44.

49 Burke, *Philosophical Enquiry*, p. 153.

50 Ibid., p. 155.

51 Ayers, *Locke*, vol. II, pp. 271–276.

52 See Peter Kivy, *Philosophies of Arts: An Essay in Differences* (Cambridge and New York: Cambridge University Press, 1997), Chapter 3.

53 Burke, *Philosophical Enquiry*, p. 160.

54 It seems clear enough that by "struck out" Burke intends "struck": that is, the fire might never have been lit.

55 In the ancient world, as my colleague, Pierre Pellegrin has pointed out to me, a "gentleman" would very likely be read to rather than read to himself, even in his own home.

56 *The New Harvard Dictionary by Music*, ed. Don Randel (Cambridge, Mass.: Harvard University Press, 1986), pp. 735 and 736.

57 T. W. Adorno, "Zur Reproduktionstheorie," in Adorno, *Zu einer Theorie der Reproduktion*, ed. Henri Lonitz (Frankfurt am Main: Suhrkamp Verlag, 2001), p. 210. I am most grateful to Max Paddison for calling my attention to this passage and for supplying me with a copy of it, both in German and in his excellent translation, which I have used above.

58 See Peter Kivy, *Authenticities: Philosophical Reflections on Musical Performance* (Ithaca, New York: Cornell University Press, 1995), pp. 137–138.

59 Paul Thom, *Making Sense: A Theory of Interpretation* (New York: Rowman and Littlefield, 2000), p. 62.

60 See Kivy, *Authenticities*, pp. 135–142.

61 The pioneering work in trying to understand this logical distinction was done by Nelson Goodman in *Languages of Art*.

62 Gregory Currie, *The Nature of Fiction* (Cambridge: Cambridge University Press, 1990), p. 98.

63   Ibid., pp. 94–95.

64   See Kendall L. Walton, *Mimesis as Make-Believe: On the Foundations of the Representational Arts* (Cambridge, Mass.: Harvard University Press, 1990).

65   Currie, *The Nature of Fiction*, p. 18.

66   Ibid.

67   William Irwin, *Intentionalist Interpretation: A Philosophical Explanation and Defense* (Westport, Conn.: Greenwood Press, 1999), p. 17.

68   Andrew Kania, "Against the Ubiquity of Fictional Narrators," *Journal of Aesthetics and Art Criticism*, 63 (2005), p. 53.

69   *The Dialogues of Plato*, vol. II, p. 656.

70   Ibid.

71   Ibid., p. 657.

72   Edward T. Cone, *The Composer's Voice* (Berkeley, Los Angeles, and London: University of California Press, 1974), p. 160.

73   Goodman, *Languages of Art*, p. 114.

74   Ibid.

75   Barbara Herrnstein Smith, "Literature as Performance, Fiction and Art," *Journal of Philosophy*, 67 (1970), p. 556.

76   Ibid.

77   Richard Shusterman, "The Anomalous Nature of Literature," *British Journal of Aesthetics*, 18 (1978), p. 320.

78   Ibid., p. 321.

79   Ibid., p. 320.

80   Richard Wollheim, *Art and Its Objects: An Introduction to Aesthetics* (New York: Harper and Row, 1968), p. 4.

81   Ibid., pp. 67–68.

82   Ibid., p. 68.

83   Ibid., pp. 4–5.

84   Ibid., pp. 69–70.

85   Richard Wollheim, *Art and Its Objects: Second Edition with Six Supplementary Essays* (Cambridge: Cambridge University Press, 1996), p. 167.

86   J. O. Urmson, "Literature," in *Aesthetics: A Critical Anthology*, ed. George Dickie and Richard Sclafani (New York: St Martin's Press, 1977, pp. 334–341.

87   Ibid., pp. 336–337.

88   Ibid., p. 337.

89   Ibid., p. 338.

90   Ibid., p. 339.

91   Ibid.

92   Ibid.

93   Ibid.

94   I have written at length on this aspect of musical performance in *Authenticities*, Chapter 5.

95   Paul Thom, *Making Sense*, p. 37.

96 Ibid., p. 38.
97 See Gilbert Ryle, *The Concept of Mind* (New York: Barnes and Noble, 1949), pp. 27–32.
98 Kivy, *Philosophies of Arts*, p. 125.
99 See ibid., pp. 123–126.
100 Ibid., p. 125.
101 Thom, *Making Sense*, p. 49.
102 I have not referred to music theory and analysis as "music criticism" because that description usually is taken to mean the reviewing of concerts in the popular press. A "music critic" is not the musical analogue of a "literary critic," in common linguistic usage, but a reviewer of musical performances.
103 R. G. Collingwood, *The Principles of Art* (Oxford: Clarendon Press, 1955), pp. 8–11.
104 Peter Kivy, *Authenticities*, Chapter 5.
105 Collingwood, *Principles of Art*, pp. 131–135.
106 Vladimir Nabokov, *Lectures on Literature*, ed. Fredson Bowers (San Diego, New York, London: Harcourt Brace, 1980), p. 3. I am grateful to Bruce Buxton for calling my attention to this passage.
107 I am grateful to Dom Lopes for this example, and for the challenge that this section tries to meet.
108 Arthur C. Danto, *The Transfiguration of the Commonplace: A Philosophy of Art* (Cambridge, Mass.: Harvard University Press, 1981), p. 82.
109 Ibid., p. 124.
110 Ibid., pp. 147–148.
111 Ibid., p. 148.
112 Ibid., p. 159.
113 Ibid., p. 163.
114 Ibid., p. 164.
115 *The Dialogues of Plato*, vol. I, p. 660.
116 Ibid., p. 285.
117 Ibid., p. 286.
118 Ibid., p. 285.
119 Ibid., p. 293.
120 I am grateful to Jeff Dean for raising this point and forcing me to re-think my interpretation of the *Ion* with regard to it.
121 *The Dialogues of Plato*, vol. I, p. 291.
122 Ibid., pp. 285–286. I have taken the liberty of substituting "embellish" for Jowett's "render," as it brings out the point more clearly. Trevor J. Saunders so translates it in his version. See Plato, *Early Socratic Dialogues*, ed. Trevor J. Saunders (London: Penguin Books, 1987), p. 50: "Yes indeed, Socrates, it's well worth hearing how splendidly I have embellished Homer." W. R. M. Lamb, in his translation of *Ion* for the Loeb Classical Library, gives a similar rendering: "And indeed it is worth hearing, Socrates, how well I have embellished Homer . . .." See Plato, *The Statesman, Philebus, Ion*,

trans Harold N. Fowler and W. R. M. Lamb, The Loeb Classical Library (Cambridge, Mass.: Harvard University Press; London, William Heinemann, 1962), p. 409.

123 Plato, *The Statesman, Philebus, Ion*, pp. 403–404.

124 Sections 24, 25, 26, and 28 contain material, somewhat revised, that was previously published as an article, "On the Banality of Literary Truths," *Philosophic Exchange*, No. 28 (1997–1998).

125 Peter Lamarque and Stein Haugom Olsen, *Truth, Fiction, and Literature: A Philosophical Perspective* (Oxford: Clarendon Press, 1994), pp. 324–325.

126 William James, "The Will to Believe," *Essays in Pragmatism*, ed. Alburey Castell (New York: Hafner, 1951), p. 89.

127 Martha Nussbaum, "Perceptive Equilibrium: Literary Theory and Ethical Theory," *Love's Knowledge: Essays on Philosophy and Literature* (Oxford and New York: Oxford University Press, 1992), p. 171.

128 Nussbaum, "Introduction: Form and Content, Philosophy and Literature," *Love's Knowledge*, pp. 4–5.

129 Lamarque and Olsen, *Truth, Fiction, and Literature*, p. 332.

130 Ibid., p. 333.

131 Kivy, *Philosophies of Arts*, Chapter 5.

132 I have discussed this at greater length in Peter Kivy, "Continuous Time and Interrupted Time: Two-Timing in the Temporal Arts," *Musicae Scientiae*, Discussion Forum 3 (2004).

133 Mauro Calcagno, "'Imitar col canto chi parla': Monteverdi and the Creation of a Language for Musical Theater," *Journal of the American Musicological Society*, 55 (2002), p. 424.

134 Chaim Potok, *The Book of Lights* (New York: Fawcett Books, 1982), quotation from the *Dallas Morning News*, no author or date cited.

135 Roman Ingarden, *The Cognition of the Literary Work of Art*, trans. Ruth Ann Crowley and Kenneth R. Olson (Evanston: Northwestern University Press, 1973), p. 97. I am grateful to Laurent Stern for suggesting the relevance of Ingarden to my project.

136 Ibid., p. 143.

137 Ibid.

138 Ibid., p. 303.

139 Madeleine L'Engle, back cover of Marion Zimmer Bradley, *The Mists of Avalon* (New York: Baltimore Books, 1984).

140 *The Dialogues of Plato*, vol. I, p. 274. I am grateful to my colleague, Pierre Pellegrin, for reminding me where to find this famous passage.

141 Susan Haack, *Manifesto of a Passionate Moderate: Unfashionable Essays* (Chicago: University of Chicago Press, 1998), p. 82.

142 Peter Carruthers, "On Being Simple Minded," *American Philosophical Quarterly*, 41 (2004), p. 208.

143 Daniel C. Dennett, *Consciousness Explained* (Boston, Toronto, London: Little, Brown, 1991), p. 195. I am grateful to Dennett for telling me where to find this passage, and to Kim Sterelny for calling my attention to the

whole matter. See, Kim Sterelny, *Thought in a Hostile World: The Evolution of Human Cognition* (Oxford: Blackwell, 2003), p. 165.

144 Ibid., p. 197.

145 Ibid., p. 59.

146 *The Dialogues of Plato*, vol. I, p. 291.

147 Ryle, *The Concept of Mind*, p. 47. My italics. I am grateful to Aaron Ridley for pushing me on this question, although I have stated it in a way very different from the way he did in discussion.

148 Ryle, *On Thinking*, p. 34.

149 Shusterman, "The Anomalous Nature of Literature," pp. 324–325.

150 Henry Fielding, *Tom Jones* (New York: Modern Library, 1950), pp. 190–191.

151 Ibid., p. 5.

152 This information concerning the reading of the congenitally deaf I have gleaned from websites, from a lecture by Dr. Sally E. Shaywitz and Dr. Bennett A. Shaywitz, of the Yale University School of Medicine, and from a personal conversation with Dr. Bennett A. Shaywitz. Neither Professor Sally E. Shaywitz or Professor Bennett A. Shaywitz is responsible for any use I have made of the information they have imparted to me, or for my possible misunderstanding of it.

153 Gregory Currie and Ian Ravenscroft, *Recreative Minds: Imagination in Philosophy and Psychology* (Oxford: Clarendon Press, 2002), p. 183. The data cited is from J. Cutting, "Descriptive Psychopathology," in S. Hirsch and D. Weinberger (eds.), *Schizophrenia* (Oxford: Blackwell, 1995).

154 Currie and Ravenscroft, *Recreative Minds*, p. 164.

155 Thomas Reid, *Essays on the Intellectual Powers of Man, The Works of Thomas Reid*, vol. I, p. 315.

156 Tony Pitson, "Reid on Primary and Secondary Qualities," *Reid Studies*, 5 (2001), p. 20.

157 Just how big and how mixed the literature bag is, when the word is broadly construed, can be ascertained by consulting Robert Howell's insightful article, "Ontology and the Nature of the Literary Work," *Journal of Aesthetics and Art Criticism*, 60 (2002).

158 Frank Sibley, "Why the *Mona Lisa* May Not be a Painting," Frank Sibley, *Approaches to Aesthetics: Collected Papers on Philosophical Aesthetics*, ed. John Benson, Betty Redfern, and Jeremy Roxbee Cox (Oxford: Clarendon Press, 2001), p. 121.

159 Ibid, p. 259.

160 Gregory Currie, *An Ontology of Art* (New York: St. Martin's Press, 1989), p. 7.

161 Ibid., p. 68.

162 Ibid., p. 75.

163 Ibid.

164 David Davies, *Art as Performance* (Oxford: Blackwell, 2004), p. 81.

165 Ibid., p. 210.

166 Ibid., p. 211.

167 Ibid., p. 220.

168 Ibid., p. 207.

169 Ibid., p. 221.

170 This argument is closely related to the argument purporting to show that high art is superior to mass art, which Noël Carroll has dubbed the "passivity argument." On this see, Noël Carroll, *A Philosophy of Mass Art* (Oxford: Oxford University Press, 1998), pp. 30–49.

171 The attempt to add aroma to cinema was a failure, if not a joke.

172 Of course if you load the dice you can come up with extreme counter-examples to this generalization. Obviously it is more labor intensive to watch *King Lear* than to read a dime novel.

Bibliography

Addison, Joseph. *The Spectator*. Edited by Alexander Chalmers. 6 vols. New York: D. Appleton, 1879.

Adorno, T. W. *Zu einer Theorie der Reproduktion*. Edited by Henri Lonitz. Frankfurt am Main: Suhrkamp Verlag, 2001.

Aristotle. *Poetics*. Translated by Richard Janko. Indianapolis: Hackett, 1987.

Augustine, Saint. *Confessions*. Translated by R. S. Pine-Coffin. Baltimore: Penguin Books, 1961.

Ayers, Michael. *Locke: Epistemology and Ontology*. 2 vols. London and New York: Routledge, 1991.

Baumgarten, Alexander. *Reflections on Poetry*. Translated by Karl Aschenbrenner and William B. Holther. Berkeley and Los Angeles: University of California Press, 1954.

Bradley, Marion Zimmer. *The Mists of Avalon*. New York: Baltimore Books, 1984.

Burke, Edmund. *A Philosophical Enquiry into the Origin of our Ideas of the Sublime and Beautiful*. Edited by Adam Phillips. Oxford: Oxford University Press, 1990.

Calcagno, Mauro. "'Imitar col canto chi parla': Monteverdi and the Creation of a Language for Musical Theater." *Journal of the American Musicological Society*, 55 (2002).

Carroll, Noël. *A Philosophy of Mass Art*. Oxford: Oxford University Press, 1988.

Carruthers, Peter. "On Being Simple Minded." *American Philosophical Quarterly*, 41 (2004).

Collingwood, R. G. *The Principles of Art*. Oxford: Clarendon Press, 1955.

Cone, Edward T. *The Composer's Voice*. Berkeley, Los Angeles, and London: University of California Press, 1974.

Currie, Gregory. *An Ontology of Art*. New York: St. Martin's Press, 1989.

———. *The Nature of Fiction*. Cambridge: Cambridge University Press, 1990.

Currie, Gregory, and Ian Ravenscroft. *Recreative Minds: Imagination in Philosophy and Psychology*. Oxford: Clarendon Press, 2002.

Cutting, J. "Descriptive Psychopathology." *Schizophrenia*. Edited by S. Hirsch and D. Weinberger. Oxford: Blackwell, 1995.

Danto, Arthur C. *The Transfiguration of the Commonplace: A Philosophy of Art.* Cambridge, Mass.: Harvard University Press, 1981.

Davies, David. *Art as Performance.* Oxford: Blackwell, 2004.

Dennett, Daniel C. *Consciousness Explained.* Boston, Toronto, London: Little, Brown, 1991.

Fielding, Henry. *Tom Jones.* New York: Modern Library (1950).

Gerard, Alexander. *An Essay on Taste.* 3rd edn. Edinburgh, 1780.

Goodman, Nelson. *Languages of Art: An Approach to a Theory of Symbols.* Indianapolis: Bobbs-Merrill, 1968.

Haack, Susan, *Manifesto of a Passionate Moderate: Unfashionable Essays.* Chicago: University of Chicago Press, 1998.

Hansen, Jette Barnholdt. "From Invention to Interpretation: The Prologues to the First Court Operas Where Oral and Written Culture Meet." *The Journal of Musicology*, 20 (2003).

Howell, Robert. "Ontology and the Nature of the Literary Work." *Journal of Aesthetics and Art Criticism*, 60 (2002).

Ingarden, Roman. *The Cognition of the Literary Work of Art.* Translated by Ruth Ann Crowley and Kenneth R. Olson. Evanston: Northwestern University Press, 1973.

Irwin, William. *Intentionalist Interpretations: A Philosophical Explanation and Defense.* Westport: Greenwood Press, 1999.

James, William. *Essays in Pragmatism.* Edited by Alburey Castell. New York: Hafner, 1951.

Kania, Andrew. "Against the Ubiquity of Fictional Narrators." *Journal of Aesthetics and Art Criticism*, 63 (2005).

Katz, Jerrold. *Realistic Rationalism.* Cambridge, Mass.: MIT Press, 1998.

Kivy, Peter. *Authenticities: Philosophical Reflections on Musical Performance.* Ithaca, New York: Cornell University Press, 1995.

——. "Continuous Time and Interrupted Time: Two-Timing in the Temporal Arts." *Musicae Scientiae*, Forum 3 (2004).

——. *The Fine Art of Repetition: Essays in the Philosophy of Music.* New York: Cambridge University Press, 1993.

——. *Introduction to a Philosophy of Music.* Oxford: Clarendon Press, 2002.

——. "On the Banality of Literary Truths." *Philosophic Exchange*, 28 (1997–1998).

——. *Philosophies of Arts: An Essay in Differences.* Cambridge and New York: Cambridge University Press, 1997.

Lamarque, Peter, and Stein Haugom Olsen. *Truth, Fiction, and Literature: A Philosophical Perspective.* Oxford: Clarendon Press, 1994.

Levinson, Jerrold. *Music, Art and Metaphysics: Essays in Philosophical Aesthetics.* Ithaca, New York: Cornell University Press, 1990.

Lindhardt, Jan. *Tale og skrift: To kulturer.* Copenhagen: Munksgaard, 1987.

Locke, John. *An Essay Concerning Human Understanding.* Edited by Peter H. Nidditch. Oxford: Clarendon Press, 1975.

Nabokov, Vladimir. *Lectures on Literature.* Edited by Fredson Bowers. San Diego, New York, London: Harcourt Brace, 1980.

Nussbaum, Martha. *Love's Knowledge: Essays on Philosophy and Literature*. Oxford and New York: Oxford University Press, 1992.

Palmer, Frank. *Literature and Moral Understanding: A Philosophical Essay on Ethics, Aesthetics, Education, and Culture*. Oxford: Clarendon Press, 1992.

Pitson, Tony. "Reid on Primary and Secondary Qualities." *Reid Studies*, 5 (2001).

Plato. *The Dialogues of Plato*. Translated by B. Jowett. 2 vols. New York: Random House, 1937.

——. *Early Socratic Dialogues*. Edited by Trevor J. Saunders. London: Penguin Books, 1987.

——. *The Statesman, Philebus, Ion*. Translated by Harold N. Fowler and W. R. M. Lamb. The Loeb Classical Library. Cambridge, Mass.: Harvard University Press; London: William Heinemann, 1962.

Potok, Chaim. *The Book of Lights*. New York: Fawcett Books, 1982.

Randel, Don (ed.). *The New Harvard Dictionary of Music*. Cambridge, Mass.: Harvard University Press, 1986.

Reid, Thomas. *Thomas Reid on Logic, Rhetoric and the Fine Arts: Papers on the Culture of the Mind*. Edited by Alexander Broadie. University Park: Pennsylvania State University Press, 2004.

——. *The Works of Thomas Reid*. Edited by William Hamilton. 2 vols. Edinburgh: James Thin, 1895.

Ryle, Gilbert. *The Concept of Mind*. New York: Barnes and Noble, 1949.

——. *On Thinking*. Edited by Konstantin Kolenda. Totowa, New Jersey: Rowman and Littlefield, 1979.

——. *Plato's Progress*. Cambridge: Cambridge University Press, 1966.

Saenger, Paul. *Space Between Words: The Origins of Silent Reading*. Stanford: Stanford University Press, 1997.

Shusterman, Richard. "The Anamalous Nature of Literature." *British Journal of Aesthetics*, 18 (1978).

Sibley, Frank. *Approaches to Aesthetics: Collected Papers on Philosophical Aesthetics*. Edited by John Benson, Betty Redfern, and Jeremy Roxbee Cox. Oxford: Clarendon Press, 2001.

Smith, Barbara Hernstein. "Literature as Performance, Fiction and Art." *Journal of Philosophy*, 67 (1970).

Sterelny, Kim. *Thought in a Hostile World: The Evolution of Cognition*. Oxford: Blackwell, 2003.

Thom, Paul. *Making Sense: A Theory of Interpretation*. New York: Rowman and Littlefield, 2000.

Urmson, J. O. "Literature." *Aesthetics: A Critical Anthology*. Edited by George Dickie and Richard Sclafani. New York: St. Martin's Press, 1977.

Walton, Kendall L. *Mimesis as Make-Believe: On the Foundations of the Representational Arts*. Cambridge, Mass.: Harvard University Press, 1990.

Wittgenstein, Ludwig. *Zettel*. Translated by G. E. M. Anscombe. Edited by G. E. M. Anscombe and G. H. von Wright. Berkeley and Los Angeles: University of California Press, 1975.

Wollheim, Richard. *Art and Its Objects: An Introduction to Aesthetics.* New York: Harper and Row, 1968.

——. *Art and Its Objects: Second Edition with Six Supplementary Essays.* Cambridge: Cambridge University Press, 1996.

——. *Painting as an Art.* Princeton: Princeton University Press, 1987.

Index